GHOSTS
of Gettysburg

VII

Spirits, Apparitions and Haunted
Places of the Battlefield

by
Mark Nesbitt

Second Chance Publications
Gettysburg, PA 17325

To Phyllis

My favorite mother-in-law

CONTENTS

ACKNOWLEDGMENTS

I am indebted to the following individuals for generously sharing their personal experiences, which appear in this volume. Krista Ardery, Tom Bowman, Craig Caba, Rob Conover, Bob Coullier, Kay Marie Le Crone, Laine Crosby, Scott Crownover, Sheri Ferguson, The Gettysburg Battlefield Preservation Association, Ann Griffith, Jennifer Henise, Nancy Householder, Jim Jacobs, Sandy Kime, MJ Kolba, Frank May, Suzanne Merkey, Peter Monahan at the Quality Inn at Lee's Headquarters, Helen Myers and her son Brian, Jack and Maria Paladino at the Cashtown Inn, Michael J. Passero, Sr., Bob Peck and Judy, Julie Pellegrino, Jeff Prechtel, Fr. Dan Ressetar, Jeff Ritzmann, Sgt. Larry Runk, Cathi Schue, Connie Solano, Dave Steele (for a story I used in *Ghosts of Gettysburg VI*—Thanks!) Lois Szymanski, Todd and Christine Thomas at the Doubleday Inn, Bill Verity, Timothy L. Vigorito, Patty Wilson.

And I would be completely remiss if I didn't thank my wife Carol for her patience in dealing with me, and her hard work in getting *Ghosts of Gettysburg VII* ready for e-publication and print.

INTRODUCTION

The sciences, each straining in its own direction, have hitherto harmed us little; but some day the piecing together of dissociated knowledge will open up such terrifying vistas of reality, and of our frightful position therein, that we shall either go mad from the revelation or flee from the deadly light into the peace and safety of a new dark age.

–H. P. Lovecraft

Much has happened in the field of paranormal studies since I wrote Ghosts of Gettysburg in 1991. Cable television programs touting "ghost hunting" have blossomed, throwing the field of paranormal studies into popular culture and prompting countless "water-cooler" debates during work hours. Millions watch "Ghost Hunters," "Ghost Adventurers," "Paranormal State," and specials such as "Mysterious Journeys," the program in which my team was featured on the Travel Channel. But, in spite of the popularity and high profile of these programs, one must ask, how far has the field of paranormal studies advanced?

Actually, the field has advanced incredibly since my first foray into it collecting stories in the 1970s. Most advances in technology, theory, and practice, however, are not shown on television due, no doubt, to several demands, not the least of which is ratings. Time constraints of a 30 minute, commercial-laced format force Jason and Grant (among others, including myself and my team) to compress an investigation of a "target rich environment" from what should be several days with return visits, into something more compact and less revealing. Project editors cut and paste dialogue and scenes to their own vision, and much raw, but important, footage (and verbiage) is found on the proverbial "cutting room floor." The caveat is obvious: television is not where the real work in paranormal studies is being done. Sadly, with the way things are, you may never see the advances which draw us closer and closer to the dead and allow us to begin rudimentary communications with those whom we will inevitably join in the Other World.

Much has happened in my personal study of the paranormal since 1991. Before that, I was merely an historian, chronicling the folklore of the area as I had heard it after several years as a park ranger, and several more as a writer. But, as happens to anyone who is the least bit curious, one thing led to another. I started attending paranormal investigations—"ghost hunts," if you will—when the (then) experts came to Gettysburg. The battlefield (which, to many people's surprise, includes the town), is one huge laboratory for the study of the paranormal. The events of the past created the "perfect storm" for a haunting: Up to 51,000 casualties in just three days; concentrated physical and emotional trauma surpassed only a few times in the history of humankind; immediate, sudden destruction of the physical bodies of soldiers so quickly that realization of their own deaths could not be comprehended; hasty burial by the thousands in unsanctified graves; inadvertent desecration of those graves by farmers or later developers; and the realization that between 800 and 1,300 bodies are unaccounted for, strewn below the manicured fields of the National Park, or between the buildings and playing fields of the college and seminary, or forgotten in back yards of the town itself. While the physical carnage ended nearly a century-and-a-half ago, the carnage to the spirits of these brave men continues.

So practically anywhere I went in Gettysburg had the potential for a paranormal investigation, enough fodder to last a lifetime. But other venues called. I attempted to compile a list of all the areas I've investigated over the last few years. It filled two single-spaced pages. I have been on or conducted well over two hundred investigations, from New Orleans to Vicksburg, Mississippi, and down the east coast, collected some 1,200 stories, gathered well over 1,000 examples of "EVP"—electronic voice phenomena—and learned a great deal more about the strange but ever-present entities I wrote about unknowingly in 1991. I wrote five more *Ghosts of Gettysburg* books and two "how to/where to" Field Guides for battlefield ghost hunters. In 1994 I started the Ghosts of Gettysburg Candlelight Walking Tours®. Later, my wife Carol, daughter Katie, and I started ghost tours in Fredericksburg, Virginia, another incredibly fertile place for paranormal activity, which gave me the opportunity to compare the "Ghosts of Gettysburg," with ghosts from Virginia's Civil War battlefields. I co-wrote with Patty Wilson two books on Pennsylvania ghosts for Stackpole Books. So, to those who have been waiting for this volume, *Ghosts of Gettysburg VII*, my sincere apologies for the delay.

While I still consider the history as a prerequisite to a haunting (which is why battlefields are so rich in ghost lore), I have begun to realize that there is more to the explanation of why a place (or person) is haunted than just a violent past. In this volume, and future works, I hope to explore more of the science involved in hauntings and how things like energy (which is what ghosts—or anything, for that matter—must have to manifest), its storage and release, plays a part in ghostly experiences. I'll also talk about the role of the perceiver as well as the ghost in a haunting.

I believe now that humans have been using the wrong science to study the paranormal, and especially ghost phenomena. Since the mid-19th Century, professionals have used the field of psychology—para-psychology to be precise—to study the phenomena we cannot explain any other way. Psychology, as a social science, has to do with data-gathering and analysis to yield trends or statistics. There's nothing wrong with that approach. I've used the same techniques to analyze my own data—the stories I've collected—and have come to some interesting, if not startling conclusions. Although everyone asks, "Have you ever seen a ghost?" a sighting of a spirit entity is one of the rarest of all manifestations, comprising only about 10-11% of all my stories. A good 60% of the stories have to do with people hearing ghosts—an auditory apparition. And all the senses are involved including touch (the cold feelings people get when in a haunted area, or even a tap on the shoulder or face), smell (for example, of rotten eggs—the same smell as Civil War black powder when it was burned), and sometimes, rarely, taste, as it relates to the sense of smell.

The gathering and analysis of data can yield valuable information. But for the paranormal events to be measurable and someday repeatable, I believe we need two other scientific disciplines: neuro-biology, to find out what is happening inside the perceiver when ghost phenomena are experienced; and modern physics—quantum physics, to be precise—to find out what is happening outside the perceiver during the same phenomena. According to some scientists, there may even be a connection between the two.

Physicist Henry Stapp realized that within the human brain, the neural synapses devolve into micro-tubules so tiny they act on the atomic level. This infinitely small space can act on the quantum level. (The term "quantum leap" had been misleadingly used to indicate a huge step forward in development; actually "quantum" refers to something infinitely tiny, on the atomic or sub-atomic scale.) This means that the human brain has the capacity to detect events that cannot be seen or heard—such as anything detected by extra-sensory perception.

Valerie Hunt, in her book *Infinite Mind,* expands this concept to include not just the brain, but also virtually every cell in the body, making human beings one big antenna for quantum events.

There are many interesting concepts that have evolved in quantum physics that relate directly to the paranormal, although many of the authors of the physics texts haven't made the connection.

Most modern scientists concede that there are probably parallel worlds existing simultaneously with ours, yet invisible. Others, like Hunt, believe there is a vast "field" which permeates everything on all levels and can act as a medium for such things as paranormal events, like "hands-on healing." Just as being able to tune into a radio station is needed to listen, experiencing those other worlds via the "field" may merely be a matter of tuning our minds into their frequency using a consciousness trained to do so. When someone runs into a ghostly Civil War soldier at Gettysburg, have they simply, perhaps inadvertently, tuned into that invisible field's frequency?

There is the conceptual theory that reality is being exercised on what physicist Lisa Randall calls "branes." The idea is that there are multi-dimensional "slices" upon which we (and seemingly other realities) exist. These branes are apparently not necessarily rigid but can flex, like a sheet of rubber with a baseball thrown into it. If two branes flex enough and touch, can they break each other's planes and one reality temporarily enter the other? Could the past reside on one of these branes? The real question is how do we control these phenomena so that we can glimpse into the Other World whenever we wish and spend as much time there as we'd like garnering information from those who now reside there?

And speaking of this "Other World" where the dead reside: is this the place we have heard of during all our existence as humans; is this "heaven?"

For some reason, scientists shun the study of the paranormal. I think I know why. People still use the old saw, "I don't believe in ghosts," putting ghosts into the category of "faith." Faith, of course, is the cornerstone of religion. Science and religion, ever since the Inquisition, have been like oil and water. I would like to see paranormal studies, especially the study of the afterlife, now move more to the side of science than "faith." "I don't believe in ghosts," should start to sound like "I don't believe in apples." Science, observation and the replication of experiencing "apples" should apply to ghosts, too. True scientists should want to study any unexplained phenomena. Some scientists, like Dean Radin, have already delved into the paranormal with their scientifically oriented minds. More "true" scientists like Radin, whose curiosity about our world is as keen as Newton's or Einstein's, are needed in the field of the paranormal.

Hopefully this book, and those that follow, will encourage that.

WHAT'S LEFT OF CAMP LETTERMAN

The worst is Death, and Death will have his day.

−William Shakespeare, *King Richard II, III, ii*

In the 1970s, Gettysburg National Military Park gave the figures for the number of combat troops who fought at Gettysburg as 97,000 Union troops versus 75,000 Confederates. These were always handed out by the ranger/historians with a grain of salt because precise figures for the armies of the Civil War are virtually impossible to ascertain. Muster rolls were taken one day; the next day someone got sick and the figures in the ranks changed. That is why officially a Civil War regiment was supposed to contain 1,000 men or 10 companies of 100 men each, yet the average size of a regiment at Gettysburg was about 380. It is called attrition and begins to happen on the day the men are mustered in. So the muster rolls taken on June 30, 1863, cannot really be considered accurate for the Battle of Gettysburg, which opened the very next day.

As well, these figures refer only to combat troops and not support troops who do the mundane, but vital work to keep the army supplied on their way to, during, and after the battle. Logistics and supply for an army requires an army. Teamsters, cooks, blacksmiths and wheelwrights, laborers, armorers, surgeons and orderlies and more all made up the support troops for the combat troops. Support troops may add tens of thousands to the numbers of combat troops.

There were also quasi-official organizations such as the Sanitary Commission and Christian Commission who followed the armies to provide for the soldiers' adjunct needs, body and spirit.

Not to mention the nebulous group of people associated with the army known as "camp followers" and "body servants." Many officers, especially in the Confederate Army, had body servants; often slaves from home, but also paid servants, to procure extra food, cook, take care of the officer's uniform and horses, and generally attend to them. Union officers had body servants, too. Sometimes they were "contraband"—escaped slaves who found their way into the Union lines and began following the Federal Army as an eventual means to escape to the North. Gettysburg hero Joshua Chamberlain had one such body servant and he mentions him in his memoirs. "Body servants" might swell the ranks of troops at Gettysburg by more than one third. Often, a small group of men (sometimes called a "mess") would hire a laundress (often a contraband) to clean for them.

"Camp followers," of course, were usually females somehow associated with the troops. Officer's wives (although they might object to the term "camp follower") visited when the armies were encamped for a while. Occasionally, a common soldier's wife would take on the disguise of a fellow soldier and accompany her husband as his "mess-mate." A few women in uniform were found dead on the field after the Battle of Gettysburg. There may have been more, unidentified because of the nature of their death-wounds. "Vivandiers," were women who accompanied the armies dressed in a particular uniform and often cared for the wounded in a semi-official role. And then there were the true "camp followers," women of dubious moral character, who have been found following every army that ever marched through history.

Once the battle was over, hundreds more non-combatants streamed to the place of carnage, to nurse the wounded or seek a relative they hadn't heard from since the fighting ended or just gawk at the dead and the blood-stained fields they left. The Sisters of Charity—nuns from nearby Emmitsburg, Maryland—and other Catholic Orders came to the battlefield at Gettysburg to do what they could. Other kind-hearted individuals were drawn to the fields and public buildings where the wounded were brought. Some regretted it.

The visions they perceived assaulted the eyes with a surreal quality. Unless you went to medical school, the average person from the 19th Century was unaccustomed to what could be so readily seen on every roadside and field into town, and on every sidewalk, street, and backyard in Gettysburg.

Headless bodies. Bodiless heads. Men cut in half. Parts of humans and pieces of bloody meat that may have once been part of a human. Hands, legs, feet, arms, some in piles waiting to be buried. Long strings of unidentifiable internal organs. All festering, after several days, in the hot July sun.

And the smells. We of the virtually odorless 21st Century have trouble imagining what things must have smelled like when people bathed perhaps once a week and most toilets were outside. Now imagine two entire armies coming into town. Soldiers aren't so domesticated when it comes to using an outhouse that may be all the way at the back of a lot, especially when the route across the yard is being peppered with minie balls. Multiply the daily excretions of each man by 200,000 for four days. Add to that the manure produced (about ten pounds per day) by 90,000 horses. Then throw in the smells of a few million pounds of meat (the 6-7,000 dead humans, the 5,000 dead horses, and the amputated limbs of the tens of thousands of wounded) rotting in the July sun and you have an assault to the olfactory nerves that defies imagining.

Perhaps this is why, on certain sultry summer nights, customers of the ghost tours return to our staff with tales of smelling on the streets a strange, antique fragrance—lilac or rose water—that hasn't been used by women since

11

American soldiers of another war began bringing exotic perfumes back from their visit to France in the early 20th Century. What could it be? they ask. If they only knew the custom of the Gettysburg ladies shortly after the battle whose nostrils were assaulted by those smells when the wind changed and blew in from the fields of carnage and their habit of carrying handkerchiefs soaked in lilac and rose water to mask the malodors.

I mention these things because they are largely glossed over during the Ranger talks on the battlefield and the presentations in the many museums in town. Another concession to the sensitivities of the modern tourist.[1]

Right after being wounded, a soldier made his way (or was carried) to an aid station immediately behind the lines, usually in a nearby woodlot for shade. A sort of triage was performed there: the bleeding was stopped, if it could be, and a doctor made a decision whether the man should be transported farther behind the lines to the field hospital for further care.

Field hospitals were usually set up in commandeered public buildings or sometimes larger private structures such as barns or homes. Some 20,000 wounded were spread all over the acres of battlefield, throughout the Lutheran Theological Seminary and Pennsylvania College buildings, and in various buildings in the town. Delivery of food and bandages was a logistical nightmare. Consolidation was recognized as the solution.

An area about a mile to the east of Gettysburg on the road to York seemed ideal. It was part of the George Wolf Farm known to locals as "Wolf's Woods" where they would picnic. It was on a rise in the terrain which afforded air movement and there was a running spring. Most convenient was the railroad, which curved to meet the road near the site to facilitate in the removal of the wounded who recovered enough to travel. Camp Letterman, named after the medical director of the Army of the Potomac, was opened around July 20, 1863, and contained from 130 to 150 tents for the wounded, surgeons, nurses, and officers. There was a cook house located near the spring. Ominously, there was a tent called the "dead house," where those who succumbed remained until they were taken to another tent: the embalming tent. Somewhere south of the camp was the cemetery.[2]

As of August 10, the camp sheltered 1,772 sufferers, but reports have as many as 4,000 passing through Camp Letterman.

Slit latrines were dug away from the camp, yet one wonders how many wounded could actually make the hike two or more times a day. The cookhouse had a special kitchen that prepared "light" dietary fare for the wounded who required it. Other than that the men were served soup, boiled beef and white bread.

Camp Letterman

Finally in November 1863, the camp saw its last patient leave. Nurse Sophronia Bucklin wrote, "The hospital tents were removed—each bare and dust-trampled space marking where corpses had lain after the death-agony was passed, and where the wounded groaned in pain. Tears filled my eyes when I looked on that great field, so checkered with the ditches that had drained it dry."

For years the fields that were "Wolf's Woods" and the site of Camp Letterman lay unused, as were the fields across the York Road. Then, in the late 1970s, modern development caught up with hallowed ground and hallowed ground lost. Name the large box store or drug store chain and they probably have a presence, along with car dealerships, restaurants, fast food stores, and numerous motels.

And that's where the trouble seems to be, paranormally speaking.

One theory as to why a place may be haunted has less to do with the structure than the ground upon which it is built. Time and again a building is found to be paranormally active and the owners are nonplussed: how can this place be haunted when it was built just a few years ago? The reason, of course, is that the structure was placed upon ground that may have a past that would lead to its being haunted. And why would ground be haunted? We know that when humans die, they release a burst of photons, what one scientist called a "light shout."[3] As well, another scientist determined that when DNA unravels—as in death—tiny bursts of nuclear energy are released. And finally, when bones are broken, there is piezoelectricity generated. Death and bones being broken are things that happen in battle when a soldier is shot. One theory is that if the geology of an area is filled with certain elements, they may "capture" the

13

burst of energy created upon death or wounding. One of the elements appears to be quartz-bearing granite—the kind of granite that is in superabundance all over the Gettysburg area.

Often, in the course of an investigation, I'll bring in a "sensitive" or medium to help with supplying names or hints as to where to go next with my questions for gathering EVP. I have three that I trust implicitly. They are not what you would expect. They don't wear bright-colored kaftans and turbans and do not carry crystal balls. They look like "soccer moms." Julie accompanied us one day out to the site of Camp Letterman to give her impressions.

Julie is a Gulf War veteran. As soon as she was on the Camp Letterman site, her paranormal sense was assaulted by horrific smells. She expressed the thought that after she left Iraq she hoped she would never smell them again: Old urine, bodily excretions, and the smell of boiling cabbage.

The smell of bodily excretions makes sense. Although the doctors at Camp Letterman were thoughtful enough to dig latrines, some of the wounded needed assistance to get to them. Often, help didn't come in time and the men simply lay in their own filth. This, no doubt, was what she "smelled."

The cabbage smell was a mystery, until a historian opined that boiled cabbage was not only a staple in the local Pennsylvania Dutch diet, but was also thought to be good for the bowels.

Julie also asked about the holes in the ground, once again seen paranormally. Why were there so many? Sophronia Bucklin may have answered that: *Tears filled my eyes when I looked on that great field, so checkered with the ditches that had drained it dry.*

Frank May is an executive for Pioneer Lines Railroad, which operates the Gettysburg and Northern Railroad freight line. But that's just what he does in the daylight hours. On his days off he is a paranormal investigator along with Rob Conover, a medium from Illinois who has been seen on the television shows, "A Haunting," and "Ghost Adventures." Several years ago, Frank, Rob, Rob's son and a friend came east. Rob had never been to Gettysburg, nor had his son. As a medium, for Rob it was more than just a visit; it was a mind-blowing, overwhelming experience.

I stood and watched as Rob began to relate what he was "seeing." A few minutes and he grew silent. I asked him what was wrong and he was speechless. "Are you on overload?" I asked. He could only nod. It was such an intense experience that he could not spend much time out on the battlefield. He quickly grew physically exhausted and we had to call it an early day. Frank, Rob and their party returned to their motel east of town, a motel that had been built upon the very ground where Camp Letterman once stood. Their day wasn't over yet.

Because of a family emergency, Frank's roommate had to leave, so Frank occupied the second floor motel room by himself. The first night he went to bed with the window closed because the weather in the early spring was still

14

cold. By morning, the window was open. Frank does not walk in his sleep and the window proved to be very noisy when he experimented with opening and closing it. How it opened without waking him up was a mystery. But not the only mystery to occur that week.

Site of Camp Letterman

During the night, he made a mental note to ask the management who was occupying the room across the hall. In the middle of the night it sounded like "someone was tearing the room apart," like they were having a party or a fight: banging on the walls, lamps being knocked over, people jumping on the beds. A maid outside his room told him that was impossible: no one had been in that room overnight. Frank hinted about his background in paranormal studies and the maid began to tell him of some strange happenings in the room across the hall from the one in which Frank heard the ruckus, the very room in which Frank was staying!

She said that some of the maids have had unexplainable experiences. They believe the second floor of the hotel is haunted. Occasionally, as they are unfolding the sheets to place on the bed, they have had the sheets violently pulled from their hands and thrown upon the floor. They had also seen an imprint on the beds that looked like a child was jumping up and down on it and have heard children's laughter coming out of thin air. As well, they've seen the sheets, after they had placed them on the bed, levitate, as if someone was under them trying to get out.

The next day was occupied with paranormal investigations of the Ghosts of Gettysburg Tour Headquarters building and the Gettysburg and Northern Railroad Engine House. It was late when they all returned to the motel. As soon as Frank entered his room he knew something was wrong. The radio alarm clock that he had set on a certain station was now set on static and was hissing ominously through the room. He turned it off and reset it to the station and the time he wanted to awaken. But other things conspired to wake him up.

He had stored his clothes in the low dresser with large drawers upon which the television sat across from the bed. In the middle of the night he heard one of the drawers slowly open, and slam shut "with a thunderous force." Since he was alone in the room, visual inspection revealed nothing. He had just begun to fall back asleep when he was awakened by something falling in the shower stall. He got up and found his shampoo on the shower floor and remembered something: although its falling didn't awaken him the night before, he found his shampoo on the shower floor that morning.

At breakfast, he began relating some of the events to Rob who just smiled. Rob said that after his son had gone to bed, he watched as the sheet lifted off his son's recumbent body as if someone unseen were pulling it in the middle. Frank related the maid's story of the same experience.

As before, their day was filled with sightseeing and investigating. Upon returning to his room, Frank's ears were again assaulted by the static hissing of the radio alarm, which had been moved off station. He re-adjusted it and picked up the phone to call Rob and tell him about it.

The phone was dead.

Frank looked around and realized that somehow it had been unplugged.

He was sound asleep when he heard it again: something crashed to the shower floor. He didn't even bother to get up and look. He also heard the bathroom door open and close. Later, he was awakened by the drawer once again slowly opening then slamming shut. A little later he was awakened again, this time by the sound of papers shuffling. All his papers were in his closed briefcase.

When he woke up he realized that the in-room refrigerator had been un-plugged and the water he'd stored in it was warm. He also noticed that overnight someone had unplugged his cell phone charger, even though he had been the only one in the room.

The maids all believe that it is the spirit of a little girl that haunts the second floor. Because of the playful nature of the paranormal events, Frank believes that as well.

First of all, if they are correct, why would a little girl haunt the site of a Civil War hospital? Was she merely playing in an area where she once visited her wounded father? Perhaps. If so, the surprising thing is, why is she not accompanied by her mother?

The other option is that Frank and the maids could be wrong about the identity of the entity. Adult spirits have been known to be pranksters. Perhaps it is one of the patients from Camp Letterman, finally freed from the constraints the wounding of his mortal body placed upon him. Perhaps now, he is finally able to roam and play and act like the young man he died as, freed by that great liberator, Death.

A NOT-SO DISTANT HEAVEN

He was a man, take him for all in all;
I shall not look upon his like again.
    –William Shakespeare, *Hamlet, Act 1, Scene ii.*

Many people who visit Gettysburg assume that the ghost phenomenon is relatively new. But the stories go back to well before the battle.

I remember the first ghost story I heard about Gettysburg. I was probably about fourteen or fifteen years old. I was hanging around the pool at the Gettysburg Motor Lodge, which, next to touring the battlefield, was my second most favorite thing to do in Gettysburg in my tourist days. I was talking to one of the lifeguards and asked if there were any ghosts associated with Gettysburg. The only haunted place she knew of was an old cemetery on Solomon Road. I can't remember any details about the story—my memory, without taking notes—was apparently no better then, than it is now.

It wasn't until I became a Park Ranger that I began hearing more ghost stories about the individual historic houses on the park and stories from the older rangers who had patrolled the National Park roads for decades before I got there. I became aware of stories that pre-dated the battle, such as the lost hunters in Devil's Den who were led to safety by a mysterious stranger who disappeared when they tried to thank him. Of course there is the very first ghost story of the battle.

On the night of July 1-2, 1863, when the Union Army's Fifth Corps was roused from its camps just west of Hanover to begin their night march toward the battlefield, a strange horseman was seen leading the column. The men would just catch up to him and he would ride ahead into the darkness. Little by little they could determine a few things about him: First, he was obviously an experienced rider from the way he carried himself upon his horse; second, he was a military man, for he wore a uniform. There was just one problem. It was the uniform of a previous war: a long cape, knicker-length pants, and a tri-corn hat, a uniform from the American Revolution. Finally, some of the men felt they recognized the figure: It was George Washington himself, Father of his Country, leading them into battle and they took it as an omen of victory. The only problem was Washington had been dead some 64 years….

But making sure a ghost story really happened is an art unto itself. Some are secondary or tertiary sources: "My uncle swore he heard this from a guy who said it happened to his friend...." Other stories have to be classified as urban legends. One of the most famous is the story of the hitchhiker.

A young man was driving home late one night (in some versions it is storming) when he saw a young woman walking along the road, dressed as if she had just been to a formal. He stopped and picked her up. He drove her to where she said she lived. He offered to walk her to her door, but she said she could make it from here. He gave her his sports jacket as protection against the rain. As she stepped out of the car in front of her house, he drove off. The next morning he returned to her house to pick up his jacket. When an older woman answered the door, he explained the situation from the night before and the woman began to cry (or screams and faints, depending on the version). She explained to him that her daughter had been killed in a car accident on that very road ten years ago. Last night was the anniversary of her death. According to one version, she tells him she's buried in the cemetery just down the road. He goes to see, and his jacket is hanging across her tombstone.

No doubt your town has one or more versions of this story. While the original tale may be true, it has suffered from embellishment, for virtually no one can resist spicing up a good ghost story.

Unless it has happened to you. It seems that no matter how many times a person tells about a personal ghost encounter, virtually nothing changes.

Once I wrote *Ghosts of Gettysburg,* the stories began to pour in. People who had experienced a ghostly encounter on the battlefield or in the town, thinking they were the only one to have experienced anything and not wanting to be ridiculed, were simply afraid to tell anyone about the event. One individual waited 57 years to reveal what happened to him one dark night on the Gettysburg Battlefield. It also has to do with a stranger along the side of the road, but contains none of the embellishments of an urban legend.

In 2000 I received a letter from a man who recounted an event that happened to him in his youth. He had just gotten out of high school and had started delivering for a family-owned plaster shop in Scranton, Pennsylvania. The shop produced figurines that were painted and sold to vendors at carnivals and fairs. He remembers the day as a bright, sunny day in July or August 1943. He had loaded up his truck and drove to a carnival some five or ten miles "the other side" of Gettysburg. He had completed his deliveries, collected the money and eaten some supper. To be fresh for the long drive back to Scranton, he decided to catch a few winks and arranged for a vendor to knock on the truck door at 10:00 P.M. to awaken him for the trip to Scranton. After rising, he swallowed a couple of cups of coffee and began his journey.

It was a warm, starry, moonlit night, perfect for his drive. He recalled that both driver's and passenger's side windows were open. Soon he arrived in the vicinity of Gettysburg. The fields on either side of the road were covered with the most beautiful layer of grass he had ever seen. He knew Gettysburg was the site of a great Civil War battle, but, not knowing anything about it, didn't realize he was driving that night, through one of the areas of combat that once cast off human souls like dust from a soldier's tunic. The lovely summer nights in Gettysburg—especially back before the 1950s tourism boom—belied the horror-filled legacy of the farm fields that once drank up the blood of young men and boys.

It is impossible to know just what road the young man was travelling on that strange night. But at Gettysburg, does it matter? Death took men in its most creative manner everywhere near Gettysburg, from instant decapitation by an artillery shell, to slowly dying from blood poisoning over an agonizing few weeks; from being instantly liquefied by canister at ten paces, to seeing one's own entrails suddenly strewn across that beautiful grass. And those who survived the battle came back during the numerous reunions as old, older and very old men. What drew them? What was it that compelled them to return to the site of the most traumatic event in their lives? It was camaraderie, no doubt, with their fellow survivors of the battle. But was there, as well, a strange camaraderie with the dead? How they saw the battlefield through eyes that had seen the horrors of the battle, we'll never know. How they could stand to return, after what they had seen, is yet another mystery of Gettysburg. But return they did until there were no more left to return and could themselves come back again only as ghosts....

He said he first became aware that he was on a battlefield when, through the darkness, he began to see shapes of markers and what appeared to be gravestones, though many people confuse some of the smaller regimental markers or flank markers for tombstones. He also noticed that the grass seemed to come right up to the edge of the highway without any ditches along the side. Suddenly, his headlights illuminated a person walking along the darkened road on the passenger side of the truck. Thinking the person needed a ride, he pulled up a little ahead of the person and stopped the truck. He realized that it was a very old man with a gray beard, dressed in gray pants, a blue shirt and wearing suspenders. The old man came up to the passenger's side of the truck, leaned close to the door and asked what time it was. The young driver turned on the cab lights, looked at his watch, and turned to tell the old man—who had vanished.

The young man slid over to the passenger side and looked out the window using a flashlight he kept in the cab, thinking that the poor old fellow had fallen. But there was no one on the ground. He exited the truck and looked under it to no avail. He flashed his light all around but could see no one. He also noticed that there were no monuments behind which someone could hide. He was stunned, but only for the time it took for him to realize exactly what it was that he had encountered. He quickly got back into the truck and sped away. As he wrote, "For the first time in my life, here was one scared 18 year old man."

Shortly after, he quit the job and joined the wartime U. S. Navy. But the experience at Gettysburg never left him. "On many a lonely night's watch out at sea, my memories go back to that night." He reflected that what he had seen, "was no human, but a soul from the past, trying to find peace and rest."

Cannon at Pickett's Charge

ALL THE KING'S HORSES

Where art thou gone, old friend and true,
What place hast thou to fill?
For it may be thy spirit form,
Somewhere is marching still.
–Rev. Nathaniel Butler, on the death of a warhorse of the 16th Maine.

East Cavalry Field is an almost unknown, forgotten part of the Gettysburg Battlefield, and yet the fighting out there made widows and orphans as sure as the battles for Little Round Top or Culp's Hill.

Cavalry in the Civil War, in spite of the taunt by the infantry of "whoever saw a dead cavalryman," was a most dangerous occupation.

Horses, by nature, can get spooked for no reason at all and refuse to jump a fence, tossing their rider into it, or run their rider into a low-hanging branch, or carry him into the blazing muskets of the enemy. A stumbling (or wounded) horse can roll its 1,000 pounds of bone and flesh over the rider, crushing ribs, pelvis or skull. Robert E. Lee's horse Traveller spooked at passing Union prisoners during Second Manassas, hauled his master to the ground, breaking both Lee's hands and forcing him to ride in a carriage for several important battles. Lee wasn't even mounted upon the famous horse, but merely standing next to him holding the reins.

Shamefully, at the beginning of the war Union cavalry was misused. Broken up into small contingents to act as aides to general officers, they had little opportunity to square off as large units against their Confederate counterparts. As well, northern boys from Cleveland or New York or Chicago lacked the experience in the saddle of their country-raised Confederate counterparts. Rebel horsemen bragged how they would ride up next to a Union cavalryman, already uneasy in the saddle, and simply yank him from his horse. Southern boys, having ridden bareback from the time they were infants, made officers like J. E. B. Stuart instant heroes with their natural prowess. Later re-organization turned the northerners, especially after the massive battle at Brandy Station, Virginia, in June 1863, into the fighting sabers wielded by Philip Sheridan in the last years of the war.

A cavalryman's life, more so than the infantryman's, was hard work. First and foremost, he had to take care of his horse and the multitude of ailments

22

and accidents to which horses are heir. For the cavalryman, it was awaken well before the infantry to feed, water, groom, pack and saddle up. Then, after the horse was attended to came the cavalryman's meal. A simple stone caught in a hoof at the beginning of a day's ride could cripple a horse for a week; water after oats will bloat him; and, in battle, horses make very large, fragile targets.

Instead of one weapon, as in the artillery or infantry, the cavalryman had three to master, clean and keep in working order: his pistol, his carbine, and his saber. Though cavalrymen were chided by the foot-slogging infantry for riding to battle, theirs was a far more sudden potential death as they galloped around a dark, tree-lined bend into the raised weapons of the enemy. And the frequency of battle for active cavalry was intense. For the Confederate infantry, for example, the Gettysburg Campaign was basically a three-day battle; J. E. B. Stuart's cavalry fought some twenty-two battles during the campaign.

Cavalry tactics, by mid-Civil War had become highly specialized. Cavalry could fight battles mounted, or dismount, send the horses to the rear, and fight lying flat on the ground. Cavalrymen were armed with breech-loading carbines while opposing infantry carried the muzzle-loading rifle-muskets that were loaded standing up. Cavalry's rapid rate of fire (and the small targets prone cavalrymen made) produced an extremely effective defense against attacking infantry. You just need to study Union general John Buford's outnumbered cavalrymen delaying the Confederate Army from 6:00 A.M.. to 10:00 A.M. at Gettysburg on July 1, to understand how effective the tactic was. When the cavalry got in trouble, they simply remounted and moved to a different position, or feigned a charge to delay advancing infantry.[1]

But perhaps the most frightening aspect of being a cavalryman was the mounted charge against the enemy cavalry's mounted charge: Hundreds of thousands of pounds of horseflesh approaching each other at a closing speed of about 50 miles per hour until they smash together. Horses tumbled and men fell into the swirling, chopping cauldron of sharp hooves, sabers, and falling horses' man-crushing bodies. In a mounted attack, if you were not shot, stabbed, bludgeoned, or trampled, you were extremely lucky....

On the broiling hot afternoon of July 3, 1863, about three miles east of Gettysburg, Major General J.E.B. Stuart and his Confederate cavalry division had been engaged in a growing fight since before noon with remarkably obstinate Union cavalry. In battles before Gettysburg, Stuart's troopers would have brushed aside the inexperienced Yankees. But two years of war had seasoned the blue cavalry. They now stood, a potent fighting force, to contest Stuart's mission.

Despite a century of historians' speculations, no one knows exactly what that mission was. General Robert E. Lee's orders to Stuart that morning are missing, or were probably verbal. Some historians have assumed that Stuart

23

was on a sweeping "end-run" to attack the rear of the Union line at the same time Pickett's Charge was striking the front.

This is clearly false because it was virtually impossible.

First, there was rarely "H-hour" timing to attacks during the Civil War. Normally, attacks were coordinated by "listening for the sound of the guns." The problem with Lee coordinating Stuart and Pickett is that even Robert E. Lee did not know exactly when Longstreet was going to launch Pickett's Charge. Lee left it up to Longstreet, who, not wanting to launch the assault at all, left it up to his artillery commander, Colonel E. P. Alexander to let him know when the Union line was softened up enough by the artillery to assure victory.

Alexander, as it turned out, sent several messages to Longstreet, one final missive practically pleading for the assault, lest there be no artillery ammunition to back it up.

So if Longstreet didn't know when the assault was to be launched and Lee didn't know, it would have been impossible for Lee to have told Stuart in the forenoon when to strike the rear of the Union line.

As well, an examination of period maps show virtually no solid roads that run into the rear of the Union line. Stuart's cavalry would have had to cut cross-country, not exactly the thing to attempt with an entire Cavalry Corps and expect it to arrive intact and on time, coordinated with another assault.

The best guess as to what Stuart's mission was is that, after swinging around to the east he was to ride north on the Baltimore Pike (easily gained from where Stuart was by the Low Dutch Road) and increase the panic and rout that was expected if Pickett's men broke through. Or, at the least, increase the Yankees' concern for their rear and supply lines with Rebel cavalry pounding up the road from Baltimore.

But Stuart found a problem with that route: pesky Yankee cavalry blocking the way at the crossroads of the Low Dutch and Hanover Roads. They'd been playing games with him since early morning, feeling the enemy's strength, dismounting and fighting, then mounting up again to withdraw. By 2:30 P.M., the sound of the main Confederate bombardment preceding Pickett's Charge had roared for an hour-and-a-half. Stuart knew the charge had to begin very soon and he had to get moving. So he ordered a massive cavalry charge to sweep from the woods across the open fields and brush the Union cavalry from the Hanover Road/Low Dutch Road crossing. What he didn't anticipate was the reaction from the Yankee cavalry to his assault.

Instead of turning and galloping away as in earlier battles, the Union cavalry launched a charge of their own headed right for the front of the Confederate column. When the two struck witnesses said is sounded like "the falling of timber," as horses and men tumbled end-over-end. The Confederate assault disintegrated and withdrew.[2]

One of the thousands of participants in the fighting on East Cavalry Battlefield was a young, newly appointed brevet brigadier general from Michigan. His name is more synonymous with a certain battle with the Sioux in Montana, yet George Armstrong Custer was at Gettysburg, leading Michigan troopers on this field. During one of the mounted charges against the Confederates, Custer with his red neckerchief, was conspicuous at the head of the pounding blue column, standing in his stirrups, waving his saber and shouting, "Come on, you Wolverines!"

Custer, prior to his appointment as one of the youngest brigadier generals ever, was known for his somewhat disheveled appearance, no doubt caused by his constant scouting for and desire to impress General George B. McClellan: Fording rivers and scouting the enemy were a dirty business. Once he gained his generalship, however, his dress radically changed: at Gettysburg he wore a velveteen jacket with gold braid looping around the sleeves and a dark-blue naval shirt with a huge collar. He sported a bright red cravat, broad-brimmed soft hat in the Confederate style, and high top boots. Most striking was his long, curly, reddish hair that he wore in ringlets nearly down to his shoulders and scented with a particularly fragrant pomade.[3]

Before he rode with the Seventh Cavalry to that fated rendezvous at the Little Bighorn in Montana, he cut his flamboyant hair. It was a good thing, too, for long, red, scented hair would have been just the thing to attract Sioux Indians to a corpse. Reports reveal that, although his body had been ritually mutilated by the Sioux (probably the women), he was not scalped.[4]

A number of years ago I received a letter from a woman in New Jersey. Obviously well-lettered, she recounted an experience at East Cavalry Battlefield that seems to have broken through this thin veil between our world and the world of Civil War soldiers now long dead.

She had been visiting Gettysburg since the early 1970s, but discovered my books in 1993 and became aware of the supernatural aspects surrounding the battlefield and town. Like many of the people who write to me with unexplainable tales, she had never experienced anything of the paranormal at Gettysburg before, but admitted that the place does have a "special atmosphere." As she wrote, "From the time of my first visit, I'd felt the presence of some awesome and almost tangibly tragic energy. If there is such a thing as the past co-existing with the present in some parallel universe, I could well believe that any boundaries between the two would overlap at Gettysburg."

She would not be the first to experience at the cavalry battlefield the dissolution of the thin veil that lies between those who stand in this world and those who cohabitate the Other World. Nor would she be the last…

She was touring East Cavalry Field for the first time with her mother. They drove in from the Hanover Road visiting the Union side of the battlefield first. They stopped at one of the first monuments to the Union Cavalry, got out of the car and began to walk toward it. "Midway on our walk to the monument, I was surprised by the scent of cinnamon." She described it as extremely strong, as if someone next to her were wearing perfume, yet neither she nor her mother use perfume. She looked to the ground for anything that might be emitting a scent, perhaps a discarded bottle or spray can, even flowers, but there was nothing. Before the daughter mentioned anything, her mother suddenly said, "I smell cinnamon!" providing an independent confirmation.

They thought maybe someone was baking at the Rummel Farm, but it was nearly a mile away and there was no breeze. Her mother was the first to suggest, in a joking fashion, that it may have a supernatural origin and asked if her daughter recalled any Civil War story that involved cinnamon. That reminded the woman that she'd read somewhere that cinnamon was a scent used in Victorian era men's hair treatments. As they walked back to their car, the odor slowly dissipated.

Michigan Cavalry Shaft in Background

Their next stop was the Michigan cavalry shaft near the spot where Custer's "Wolverines" crashed into Stuart's rebels. They began to read the inscription on the monument and…there it was again. Stepping back to view Custer's sculpture, they were hit with the full scent: cinnamon.

They proceeded to the next stop on the tour, still puzzled as to the strange origin and disappearance of the scent, which now, near the New Jersey monument, was completely gone. Then her memory kicked in: she had read about Custer in a popular book and remembered that after graduation from West Point, he began to grow his hair long and use, as was the style of the era, a spice-scented pomade. He used so much of it that his friends gave him the nickname, "Cinnamon."

In her letter she pondered some of the same unanswered questions all seekers of the bizarre and otherworldly ponder. Since few people even know that Custer was at Gettysburg, but "Custer's Last Stand" is legendary in American History, why might his ghost make its presence known in an out-of-the-way place such as East Cavalry Field? She had never been to the battlefield monument at the Little Bighorn in Montana, but had been to Custer's grave at West Point, New York, and found it a "scenic, serene place, probably too peaceful for ghosts." She also recalled that, according to some historians, "little, if any, of his [Custer's] remains were recovered after initial burial at the Little Big Horn." Perhaps it's no wonder then, that she detected no cinnamon scent at his grave.

Most people think that the only way to experience a ghost is by seeing one. Therefore, when one of the other senses is high-jacked by the supernatural, individuals will somehow ignore it, or make excuses for it. The actual sighting of a ghost comprises only about 10% of all my collected stories. Far more common is the auditory experience: footsteps crossing the floor or coming down the stairs when there is no one visible to make the noise; or as in the case of a woman who lived near East Cavalry Field, the sound, in the dark of night, of a column of horses trotting by; when she arose to look out the window to see from where the sound came, there were no horses or riders to be seen. But all the senses are involved, especially the sense of smell. Often, modern tourists walking down the streets of Gettysburg in this century will get a whiff of rosewater—outdated perfume of the 19th Century—with which the women of Gettysburg, after the battle, soaked their handkerchiefs as a defense against the smell of rotting corpses in the streets and fields. The smell of rotten eggs is sometimes detected on the battlefield, with the individual not realizing that sulfur was one of the main components of black powder, the main propellant for firearms of the Civil War. Generic smells are one thing. But more distinct and rare smells may be proof of a long-dead presence whose ghost can be identified. And yet, as rare as those visual presentations of the supernatural are, still there are those who have seen....

Police, doctors and nurses are some of my favorite people from which to glean a ghost story. Like a few other segments of our society, they are trained observers who, often subconsciously, will pick up on the smallest details of an event. Writers and artists can be placed into that same category of trained observers.

I first met Jeff Prechtel while working with his father, Don, a gifted and accomplished military artist whose works hang in some very prestigious board rooms and museums. Don and Jeff were the two artists I was accompanying a number of years ago through the Triangular Field, taking documentary photos for an upcoming painting Don was working on. Suddenly, in the field known for a higher than average camera failure rate, my camera stopped working. I looked over at Don and his camera had jammed as well. Twenty yards beyond him, Jeff was fiddling with his camera, attempting to get it working again. Don was gracious, admitting that the ghosts had won that day. As we drove away from the once blood-spattered ground, Jeff called from the back seat that his camera was functioning again. Don handed his camera back and within a few seconds, it too was working. By the time we got back to town, mine was operating as well.

Some fifteen years later, Jeff himself has become a talented artist. His passion for the American Civil War has continued and he visits Gettysburg from his home in the northwest whenever he can. He is familiar with the fine details of Civil War uniforms as only one who needs to paint them can be. As well, he has been a reenactor and so is intimate with the nuances of both Union and Confederate uniforms. His encounter with the unexplainable occurred during the 130th Anniversary of the battle in 1993.

3rd Pennsylvania Cavalry Monument

He, his father and three other reenactors, all dressed as Confederates, had travelled out to East Cavalry Field one evening. Jeff remembered the air was clear since the heavy thunderstorms of the day before and the evening shadows were lengthening. He and his father had approached one of the monuments to the Union Cavalry near where they'd parked their van; their three friends had walked farther out on the battlefield. Jeff was standing looking toward a distant tree line while his father snapped photos behind the monument. In the distance he noticed a figure standing alone in the field. His reenactor's eye caught that the young man wore kersey trousers and a light colored shirt and had a kepi pulled low over his eyes. Jeff assumed it was the teenage son of one of his two friends who had come with them and he waved and called to him to return to the van since they were ready to leave for dinner. To his annoyance, the young man just stood transfixed, silently staring back at him, acting like a dismounted cavalry picket on the qui vive for the enemy.

Jeff continued to motion and yell, frustrated by the young man's absolute refusal to even acknowledge his presence. Just as he was about to holler again, one of the friends came up behind him and asked him at whom he was yelling. He turned and replied, "I'm yelling at Lucas to come to the van." He turned back to the open field and the figure was gone. His friend motioned over his shoulder. There, walking toward them was the other friend and his son, Lucas.

His first thought was that there had been another reenactor having a little fun with him, playing "ghost." But his artist's eye noticed that the field was flat with only some wispy Queen Anne's Lace, not enough to afford cover for a human being, even lying down. The tree line was far too distant for someone to have reached in the second or two his gaze had been diverted. An hallucination? If so, it was real enough for him to call out to what he thought was his friend's son, real enough for him to grow frustrated when he was ignored. It was real enough for him to be perplexed at its sudden disappearance.

A few weeks later while looking at the photos his father had taken, it suddenly made sense to him. "Somehow we had pierced that great mystery, bending time, and somehow touched the past," he wrote. He wondered if, during their visit dressed as the Confederate "enemy," they had awakened a guardian of the fallen Federal cavalrymen, a spirit still trapped by his sense of duty and protective of the monument and ground where his comrades fought and fell.

Like most of those who have experienced one of the Ghosts of Gettysburg, Jeff's letter ended not with certainty, but with a question: "Had one of their compatriots travelled back across that darkened veil to protect what he felt compelled to protect those 130 years before?"

ANOTHER DESCENT INTO HELL

Are we monstrously trapped in the natural flux,
as are the seasons, suns and moons?
Are we to counterfeit, over and over,
from death to rebirth, our ancient sins?
Are we doomed to repeat this dreary life,
over and over and over, forever and anon?

During the battle, Pennsylvania Hall on the Gettysburg College (then known as "Pennsylvania College") campus was used, as was virtually every large structure in Gettysburg, as a hospital for the wounded. It is pretty much agreed that the lower floors were used as the operating areas, and the upper floors for recovery rooms. We know this partially because of the descriptions of visitors to the hospitals. They described seeing from a distance, strange "pyramids" underneath the windows on the first floor, which sometimes reached up to the sills. Upon approach, they would have been repulsed by the hideous realization that these pyramids were actually made up of hands and feet, arms and legs, amputated within the building and tossed ignominiously out the windows to land with a sickening, liquid "thump" on the pile. Overworked orderlies occasionally would arrive with wheelbarrows, load the disgusting, oozing mess, which by then would have begun to putrefy in the July heat, and haul the once precious cargo away to be buried, or perhaps burned. This is why, years ago, while I was researching Brua Hall, the theater building just across the "quad" from Pennsylvania Hall, I had to agree with one of the professors who said he thought Brua Hall was built upon a graveyard. A graveyard, yes, but only of certain pieces of men's bodies.

If one were to choose one story from the collection of hundreds in my files to represent the most fascinating, the most fabulous, most frightening supernatural experience, it would have to be the plight of two Gettysburg College administrators as they were attempting to make their way out of Pennsylvania Hall via an elevator which transported them, most reluctantly, to the Hell on earth of a Civil War hospital in the cellar of the structure.

It is fascinating because I knew the administrators and security people involved, all solid, down-to-earth individuals, none prone to hallucinations or fabrication. It is fabulous (in the old sense of the root word "fabled"), in that it has virtually become a legend. It is frightening, because it contains all the earmarks of horror: It happened late at night; there is total revulsion of what lies just before the participants as the doors of the elevator slowly open—dead and dying men, suffering amputations and worse; and there is literally no escape from the vile and hideous scene—no matter how many times they press the buttons to take them up, the elevator remains frozen; the scene is out of time but not quite out of reason—the place had been used for just the purpose they were witnessing...although 120 years previous; and, worst of all, they may be forced to join in, as a grizzled, ghostly orderly begins to approach and beckon them into his world.

It is a story that is almost too good to be true.

And for those that doubt it is true, I have another story....

I was autographing books at the Gettysburg College Bookstore a few years back. A young couple came up and purchased *Ghosts of Gettysburg III*, and *Ghosts of Gettysburg IV*. They said that they already owned the first book. The man leaned a little closer and said, "You know, your elevator story? We're friends with the woman that happened to."

I was interested that these two strangers and I had a mutual friend, "Oh," I said. "Then you know..." and I mentioned the names of the two participants in my original story. The puzzled look on their faces was disturbing.

"No. We've never heard of those people. Our friend's name was..." and they gave me a completely different name.

At first I was confused. "That's not the name of either of the people I wrote about."

The looks on their faces were just as adamant. They knew this woman personally; she was a solid, upright individual. She wasn't the type to make things up.

I asked them what she had told them.

She had been working for an accounting firm out of Lancaster, Pennsylvania. They were doing an audit at Pennsylvania Hall, the administration building for Gettysburg College. Someone had asked her to go to the car and get some papers. She got in the elevator. The elevator malfunctioned and, instead of stopping at the first floor, descended into the basement—and into a scene she was not prepared for: men being sliced up like pieces of butcher's meat by a bloody surgeon; men in dank, rust-colored corners, quivering from shock and loss of blood; orderlies carting piles of crimson limbs from operating table to weltering corners, dark and slick with blood.

I asked them if they were still friends and they said yes. I asked if she still lived in Lancaster. They said no, she lives in Denver, Colorado. Did they mind if I called her? They gave me her number.

A few days later I called.

She was pleasant and not reluctant to talk about her experience, although still, in her voice, was that tone that can only be described as questioning as to what exactly had happened to her that afternoon. She repeated the story I had heard from her friends almost verbatim. She added a few details that her friends had not known about. It is my experience, after interviewing hundreds of witnesses to the paranormal, that the event leaves an indelible impression upon one's mind and is usually never forgotten until one's death…and perhaps not even then.

This, then, makes three individuals at two separate times that have experienced a descent into what would seem to be the impossible. (At this writing I am tracking down what may be a third incident involving the elevator that drops into a man-made hell on earth.) Of course, if these separate incidents were all that has happened in "Old Dorm" they would be enough to convince even the most ardent skeptic that something out of the ordinary was happening there.

Though the elevator story is, by far, the most famous, other mysterious events at Pennsylvania Hall have occurred.

I received a letter from an alumnus of Gettysburg College who lived in Pennsylvania Hall before it became the Administration building for the college. (The original students' name for Pennsylvania Hall was "Old Dorm" because that's just what it was used for—a dormitory. As this gentleman's letter attests, that was its use in the 1950s.) He was a freshman in 1954-55. His room was located on the second floor just to the right of the black iron staircase. He considered himself a skeptic, but doesn't doubt that most of those who claim to have had an encounter with the paranormal are probably telling the truth, since, in life, there are many unsolved mysteries…including one that preyed upon him periodically while he remained in the room that once housed soldiers recovering from the most desperate assaults upon their bodies and their health.

He wrote that occasionally his room was permeated with a "sickeningly sweet smell," unlike anything he had smelled before or has smelled since. The memory remained vivid nearly half a century later. He gave up trying to identify it and opined that it might be something long ago absorbed into the walls of the building "discernable within certain atmospheric conditions." He also suggested that one might suspect that the smell may have come from medicines once used in that room, or perhaps even from decomposing flesh and blood. Its connection to the sinister use his room once had, he couldn't confirm. (Perhaps the skeptic re-emerging?) But he knew it wasn't the smell of paint, fungus, cleaning liquids or waste materials. He ended with a confirmation of the indelible nature of certain powerful, yet unexplainable events: "To this day, I am haunted by the memory of that sickeningly 'sweet' smell…. I could detect that smell instantly—after nearly 50 years have passed."

Colleges seem to be natural generators of ghosts, in particular, poltergeists, or "noisy ghosts." Poltergeist activity includes doors slamming, lights flicking on and off, articles moving about as if pushed by unseen hands and even levitation—things floating through the air. The phenomenon is called psycho-kinesis and has been observed in a laboratory, and while it is attributed to the over-abundance of energy in pre-adolescent women, why wouldn't the same be true for any human with energy to spare? And, as anyone can attest who has been to college, there's plenty of energy around.

In 1994, I created walking tours based upon my *Ghosts of Gettysburg* books. The first route took our customers down Carlisle Street and through the Gettysburg College campus. Of course, "Old Dorm" was included in the tour, as was Stevens Hall, where the blue-tinged face of a young boy has been seen by female residents, floating, on cold winter evenings, outside the window. The problem is, only his head is seen, and the window is all the way up…on the third floor. He has been seen so often over the years that residents of the third floor of Stevens have named him, the "Blue Boy." Rumors from the college place his most recent sighting just a few years ago. Testimony from two customers on our Carlisle Street Tour places his appearance more recently than that….

Stevens Hall

Nearly everyone who takes our tours wants to know: Have the guides ever seen anything spooky or heard any stories of the supernatural at Gettysburg? The answer is yes, and at least one guide on our Carlisle Street Tour took the time to record a bizarre and unexplainable sighting at Stevens Hall.

During his tour he noticed a man, woman and a boy from his tour standing by the pine tree near Stevens having an animated conversation. After every other person in the tour had left, they approached the guide. The man, referring to a statement our guide had made at the beginning of the tour, asked, "You said you don't set anything up on these tours, right?" Our guide answered in the affirmative and, curious, asked if the man had seen anything. The man began to say something, then stopped and said, "No, forget it. You'll just think I'm crazy." Our guide assured him that, in our business, we hear a lot of weird things from completely sane people.

Convinced that he would not be laughed at, he began his story. While our guide was telling the tale of the "Blue Boy," he had noticed a movement in a bush at the northwest corner of Stevens Hall. He claimed that there was a face peering out from the bush. His wife concurred: she saw the same thing. Both said that it appeared to be the face of a young boy, perhaps 15 or 16 years old, and that the face had a strange bluish tinge to it. Interestingly (and perhaps a clue to the paranormal nature of the sighting), the man saw the figure from the waist up, yet his wife only saw the face. Whoever it was, he appeared to be playing "hide and seek" with them: Whenever they would look toward the bush, the indigo-tinged face would pull back into the foliage; when they looked away, he would appear again. The guide asked if they could see any style of clothing or hat. The husband said that he appeared to have some type of hat. The guide, who was dressed in period clothing, pointed to his own "slouch" hat, but the man said no, it was more like a cap. The guide was a reenactor, and the headgear the man described sounded to him like the famous short-brimmed "forage cap" so common to the American Civil War soldier.

Collectors of ghost stories are always wary of someone making something up. Because of the family's strange actions before approaching him and the man's reluctance to share the story for fear of being thought crazy, our guide was convinced of the truthfulness of his observation.

The shrub has since been removed from Stevens Hall. The ghost of the Blue Boy? Perhaps not.

HOW TO UN-HAUNT A HOUSE

...scientific study and reflection had taught us that the known universe of three dimensions embraces the merest fraction of the whole cosmos of substance and energy.

–H. P. Lovecraft

Say the word "exorcist," and most people think of the child played by Linda Blair lying in bed, her head twisting around like an owl's, vomiting green funk and cursing at the priest trying to free her from Satan's grasp. The 1971 book, *The Exorcist* by William Peter Blatty was based upon a true 1949 case of what may have been, in reality, poltergeist manifestations. When the young man (not a female as in the novel) was 13 years old, the family began hearing scratching sounds coming from within the walls of their home in Cottage City, Maryland, near Washington, D.C. An exterminator found no signs of mice or other animals. After he left, the noises grew in intensity, then changed to the sound of someone walking in the hall. Furniture in the house and china in the kitchen would move. Then the young boy became the focus of the activity.

In the dead of night his bed shook violently and the sheets were pulled from it. His parents convinced themselves that the evil spirit of a dead relative was the cause. They called in their minister, who tried praying with the boy and his parents, and the entire congregation of their church. In the name of the Father, Son, and the Holy Ghost, he ordered the entity out of the boy. While this supplication almost always works, the boy continued to be tormented. The minister offered to spend the night to continue to work with him.

During the night the minister heard the boy's bed creak and felt it vibrate. He convinced the boy to sleep in a large chair in the room, but no sooner was the boy comfortable than the massive chair began to move backward until it crashed into the wall, then rotated until it dumped the child on the floor. In the morning the exhausted minister suggested the boy be examined by psychiatrists. Suddenly, the child went wild and red scratches appeared on his skin. To the amazement of all, the scratches spelled out, "Go to St. Louis!"

The boy was sent to a hospital in St. Louis, but while there his condition worsened. Jesuit priests in St. Louis diagnosed possession and began performing exorcism rituals that lasted a week. Eventually he was declared cleared of the possession.[1]

While many people are somewhat familiar with the case (at least the fictionalized novel and motion picture) most are still confused about exorcism. Those who have had experiences in their homes want to call a person of the cloth to exorcise their dwelling. According to at least one Russian Orthodox priest, an exorcism is performed on a person; a cleansing is performed on a house.

This priest, during a telephone interview, revealed that he had been called in to perform at least one house cleansing in Gettysburg, although he could not remember exactly where. He did not think that it was the house near the Seminary that once held the young Civil War soldier captive, buried alive under a festering mass of rotting human flesh, until he lost his mind.[2] He seemed to think it might have been on Baltimore Street. Anyone who has taken our Ghosts of Gettysburg Candlelight Walking Tours® Baltimore Street Tour will realize that the house could have been any number of places along the main street in Gettysburg: The house where the melancholy young man in a Civil War uniform seems stuck in the older section of the house while college parties go on in the newer section; the renovated house where Civil War veteran "Uncle Joe" makes his presence known by sending just his shadow up the stairs; our own Ghosts of Gettysburg Tours Headquarters at 271 Baltimore Street where doors open…and close…seemingly on their own and the woman who owned the house longer than anyone, and her children, make themselves known by speaking on electromagnetic devices.[3]

Nor have any other homeowners in Gettysburg come to me to offer that their house was the subject of a cleansing. That, however, is not to say that some have not needed cleansing.

At least one Seminarian was asked to cleanse a house in Gettysburg sometime in the mid-1990s. A woman saw a lady appear in her house, then promptly vanish. This could be chalked up to one person's imagination, except that the vanishing lady was seen by others as well. "Merely" seeing a ghost in one's house, however, doesn't mean that the house needs a religious cleansing. If so, dozens of homes in Gettysburg and other cities would keep the priests busy for years to come.

And while we know by rumor and innuendo that several homes in Gettysburg have been subject to a religious cleansing of pesky, troublesome spirits, what should really alarm us are the ones which are in desperate need, but have not yet had a ritual cleansing. At least one has had a demonologist there twice. He has refused to return.

The houses need not be Civil War vintage. One house, built in the 1960s near where Confederate troops maintained a field hospital on the first day of battle, apparently contained the spirit of a woman who committed suicide there. She has been seen a number of times by her former neighbors since the incident. As well, things—books, pillows, and even heavy furniture—in adjacent houses move around when no one is home (and sometimes when there is someone home) and at least one neighbor's dog, fearful, cowering, whining to leave, will not enter the room where the suicide took place. It would appear that the spirit of the woman, perhaps feeling guilty about her deed of self-murder, certainly needs release from whatever traps her there. But in this case, it may not be the house that needs attention. Mediums would suggest that the person who committed suicide needs to be helped to "cross over"—over to the Other World.[4]

Another house near the college has been the scene of not one, but possibly two suicides, the second apparently linked to the first, or at least linked to perhaps the spirit in the house who "recommends" the young person kill themselves, or suffer some consequence. The spirit is described as wearing white and acting "mad," in the Victorian sense of the term—insane. He is seen descending into the cellar where he apparently dwells. A particularly vulnerable individual sees him, receives the directive to choose to either end their life, or join him in some bizarre communion. As if under some spell, the student chooses the former.

But of the houses that should have some sort of cleansing, one stands out. It is on York Street, near the bend where Hanover Street bears off. I was invited to do an investigation there in the spring of 1999.

The notes are sketchy. Some are in my handwriting and some in another's. They are terse, but re-reading them after all these years, their brevity and coldness seems to emphasize the haunting, supernatural events that were happening in that house. I know I made a recording of the investigation, but the tape has disappeared. Perhaps we were to return for a follow-up, although our presence probably wouldn't have made a difference, except to continue to record any additional uncanny happenings. What was needed, in this case, was a priest.

According to the notes, the investigation was done on March 15. There are references to obviously dates of a previous year: March 27; April 3. The notes in the other hand indicate that there was a particularly active period between March 12 and March 15.

Apparently someone smelled what they called "campfire smoke" inside the house. While some of the inhabitants smoked cigarettes, they recalled that it was obviously a different smell. Later they also noticed that the ceiling was "scorched." Whether the two incidents were related is not known. It wouldn't be the last time fire was involved in the haunting.

The house was typical of Gettysburg's Civil War era with smaller than normal rooms. Some speculate that the smaller rooms were more easily heated—simple body heat of three or four people will sometimes suffice to keep the smaller rooms comfortable. The modern inhabitants claimed that, even with several people in one room of the house, they would periodically feel a chill creep into the area. They also noticed that much of the activity happened during the early morning hours. They felt, for a number of reasons, that there was more than one spirit moving through the house. They would periodically hear what they described as a "clamoring" in unspecific areas in the house.

A friend had actually seen a little girl wearing a white dress standing in the room. Sometime later they saw a cushion on the couch depress.

The couch seems to be the center of much of the activity. Fire seems to be one of the tools the entity uses to attract attention. Burn holes would suddenly appeared in the couch while two of their friends were watching. There is one note that says the couch actually moved with a friend sitting on it; another note later states that "the couch levitates." This would indicate another entity besides the little girl.

From the notes of the other person:

"Fri 3-12. Noticed coats moving on back of lounge chair. Chair opens and retracts slowly, curtains are being manipulated."

"Sat 3-13. Coat again being manipulated on back of chair about 1:00 A.M. Noticed drops of fluid around chair's base. "[My notes of the incident indicated that there were two drops of what they identified as blood around the chair.] In a parenthetical note, the writer indicates that the coat was folded neatly across the top of the back of the chair, suggesting that the entity actually folded the coat and laid it neatly across the chair.

"Sun 3-14. Noise & footsteps on the steps [to the second floor] and in the kitchen. A puff of smoke out of nowhere in the living room by lamp. Strong smell of coffee. Couch levitated and moved." [Here it is indicated that a male visitor saw the little girl in the white dress standing in the room.]

"Mon 3-15. _____ [name withheld] witnessed electronic voice phenom. in TV."

My notes expand upon the EVP event. What the person actually experienced was ITC or Instrumental Trans-communication, of which EVP is a subset. ITC is when entities use other instruments such as telephones, radios or televisions to communicate with us. The television was apparently not on—in my notes, "blank." She was apparently seeing images emerge from the blank screen.

The local Radio Shack store was once located in the North Gettysburg Shopping Center on old Route 15. The shopping center was built upon what was the staging area and on the route of advance of some Confederate brigades as they attacked Barlow's Knoll on the afternoon of July 1, 1863. No doubt some of their wounded made their way back to the site since the rear is where the field hospitals are set up. Some may have died there as well. I would frequent the electronics store for equipment, tapes and batteries. The manager of the Radio Shack once told me I should plan an investigation there. On at least two or three occasions, she had opened the store first thing in the morning and heard a television babbling at the rear of the store. She knew she had been the last to close the night before and was obviously the first to open. She said she walked back to where the televisions were and the noise would fade.

She examined the devices and found that they were all unplugged. She was a witness to ITC—someone attempting to communicate from another plane using modern technology.

H. P. Lovecraft once wrote that, "Searchers after horror haunt strange, far places." In Gettysburg, those places may very well be strange, but are never very far away.

POLICING THE PARANORMAL

...join the ranks of a growing body of philosophers who believe that thought and mind precede physical substance, and that when matter disintegrates after its form has changed, the mind and soul are freed and the power of thought remains.

−Valerie Hunt, *Infinite Mind*

Some witnesses to paranormal happenings are better than others. Being able to notice and remember detail is one of the most important aspects of being a percipient to the supernatural. The problem is, a paranormal event, like seeing, hearing, or smelling something completely out of the norm, usually happens quickly; much of the analysis must be done after the event has occurred, by memory. "Did I really see that?" is usually the way we analyze a sighting. A good memory helps, but most people who have had contact with beings from "The Other World," have no trouble recalling what happened to them—it is seared into their mind. A quick decision to pay attention is the most important thing in analyzing a paranormal event, and that is why some of the best witnesses to ghostly events are doctors, nurses and police.

Time and again I've spoken to police and they have stated that there is a great deal of intuition involved in their work. A "gut feeling" about drawing their weapon before rounding a corner has saved many officers' lives. When emotions are running high, adrenaline is coursing through the system and decisions must be split-second, sometimes a feeling is all you have to go on.

It would seem like the Gettysburg Police may have a leg up on even the most dedicated paranormal investigators we see on television. They not only patrol, 24/7, the streets which witnessed the massive effusion of blood during the battle, but are called to enter many of the battle-era buildings which may still hold the spirits of those who suffered and died within them. For a policeman to enter an old abandoned building is creepy enough; to do it in Gettysburg takes some special kind of courage.

It has been my privilege to know a number of Gettysburg police officers. They have a tough job. Not only do they have to keep the 8,000 inhabitants of the borough safe, they are often called in to help the Gettysburg College security staff when the students grow rowdy. Throw in the approximately 1.6 million visitors who annually fill the borough and you understand that the

Gettysburg Police Department is a small-town law enforcement agency with big city responsibilities.

Oh. And those 8,000 residents of Gettysburg are just the living inhabitants. How many dead inhabitants roam Gettysburg is still under discussion.

Within the last few years one veteran sergeant from the Gettysburg Police Department was called out to a house on West Street and Buford Avenue. It was a typical Gettysburg duplex that sits on the foundation of a demolished Civil War era building. Neighbors had heard a woman's screams coming from inside. According to the reports, the neighbors thought she was being killed. The sergeant called another officer on the radio and told her not to enter the house alone, to wait for his back-up. As the two officers met outside the building, they heard it too: a blood-curdling scream echoing from inside.

There is nothing more dangerous for a police officer than a domestic quarrel. All too often they appear on the scene to witness a husband viciously beating his wife. They drag the man away from his bloodied spouse only to have her pull out a gun and defend her husband from the police. It is strange and inexplicable…but true. This would account for the sergeant's caution.

The sergeant took the lead and entered the side of the duplex from where they thought the scream had come. To his surprise, that side was vacant. He moved cautiously through the downstairs, checking each room, not knowing when he would come across the bloody, broken body of the woman he had just heard. To his relief, there was no one on the first floor. Now to the second floor.

Again, a cautious, apprehensive investigation revealed no foul play. Overcoming all his instincts not to, he began to climb the stairs into the attic, knowing that, if the other floors yielded no body, certainly the female victim was lying in the attic.

His flashlight made weird images through the space seemingly unchanged over the years. Hanging clothes left by numerous former tenants made eerie dancers of shadows and boxes seemed to open and close by themselves as the single light played over them. But still, to his relief, no woman's body.

Just as he was about to descend the stairs, he noticed that there was a hole broken through the wall into the other duplex. Again the adrenaline rushed as he realized that the woman whose dying screams awakened the whole neighborhood was probably there. And, perhaps her attacker, as well.

He realized that the farther he got into the house, the more the likelihood he would run into the body and probably the assailant. And, having illuminated the attic with his flashlight, whoever else was on the other side of the wall now knew he was not alone. Every gut instinct told him not to go into the other side of the building, but someone was going to have to do it, and leaving without finding the poor woman who had just screamed her life out was not an option. Carefully, he moved through the hole in the wall into the other duplex's attic.

A sweep with the flashlight revealed more dancing shadows, more boxes, some old furniture…but no body.

He began to relax a little, but knew that there were two more floors below him that needed to be searched. He started to descend the stairs, realizing that the domestic argument that led to the woman's screams may have started with the family on this side of the duplex. He opened the door from the attic into what he thought would be the bloody remnants of a domestic quarrel and walked into…an empty apartment.

Neither side of the duplex had been rented. He finished his search of the second floor, then the first. He left the building and explained the situation to an incredulous fellow-officer. Confused neighbors, expecting to see the sergeant come out with someone in handcuffs and call for the undertaker, began to slowly make their way back to their homes. There was an awkward silence between the officers, until finally, they shrugged their shoulders, re-entered their patrol cars, and drove off.

This was, after all, Gettysburg….

DARK NIGHT OF THE SOUL

O proud Death,
What feast is toward in thine eternal cell,
That thou so many princes at a shot
So bloodily has struck?

–William Shakespeare, *Hamlet*

In the Civil War, when a line of infantry was hit by artillery fire it was beyond horror: Dozens of men were bowled over like ten-pins, the remnants of their mortal forms often unrecognizable. But when artillery shelled another battery, it was a sudden descent into Hell. Horses—six to a gun—panicked and tried to tear from their harnesses. Pandemonium reigned from that moment. If a shell landed amongst the horses, the butchery was complete: One only need imagine what ten pounds of exploding iron does to the soft belly of a horse or their fragile legs. If a round landed in one of the ammunition chests, the bedlam was multiplied. When artillery shells hit, men and horses did not just sink gently to the ground, "in glorious sacrifice to the cause." Pieces of flesh were thrown into the air, whirling like bloody pinwheels and landing in a tangled welter of quivering gore. The screaming of men and horses intermingled until you could not tell one from the other, and the blast of exploding shells pounded a rhythm to the cacophony of death. Never on the drill fields of the Virginia Military Institute would young Major J. W. Latimer have seen such a sight.

Major J. W. Latimer

Nineteen-year-old Latimer was supposed to be graduating with his class at the prestigious Virginia Military Institute. But he had left the school in his sophomore year when war between the two sections of the country broke out and volunteered his services to his native South. At this moment—late afternoon of July 2, 1863—instead of holding a cherished sheepskin diploma, he was desperately fighting for his life with his artillery battalion on a hill unsuitable for artillery east of Gettysburg.

A grave responsibility it was for such a young man. Behind him rested the left flank of the entire Confederate Army of Northern Virginia. General Robert E. Lee was said to be meeting his officers at a farmhouse just behind this position. And while the Yankees had not shown the gumption to attack so far in the battle, one never knew. Latimer's artillerists—most of whom were years older than their youthful commander—composed the iron-studded outpost, discouraging any Yankee attack upon this flank.

Latimer originally placed 14 guns along the ridge that extended south from the road to Hanover, but the counterbattery fire from the Yankee batteries placed on the opposing hill with the cemetery soon made it untenable.

One artillerist thought that the Yankees already had their range before they had arrived on the ridge. Shells began crashing in on them as soon as they had gone into battery.

Still, Latimer's artillery pieces remained in their exposed position for several hours. Flanked by Union artillery, unable to hide his horses and caissons behind the hill, the young major finally asked permission to withdraw his guns, which was granted. But since he was protecting the left flank of the entire Confederate army, he chose to leave behind four guns. He would command them himself; the position was too dangerous to ask anyone else to command there. It was a decision that would cost him his life.

In the evening, Confederate infantry began an assault toward the cemetery and Latimer opened fire to support them.

While the majority of the Confederate batteries had withdrawn, the Union guns continued at full strength, now concentrating their fire at four targets instead of fourteen. The young major was wounded severely in the arm. As night was falling, Latimer gave his last orders to his battery commanders to withdraw the guns to a safe place, something he never would have done for himself.

After night fell, the farmhouse to the rear of Latimer's battle must have resembled something out of a young man's nightmares. The once tranquil home of Daniel Lady and his family had been transformed, in a matter of hours, by the hideous necessities of war into a field hospital. As he was being carried to the old stone farmhouse by gentle litter-bearers, he no doubt heard the moans and pleadings of the wounded: *Don't...please...please!...don't cut...please leave my arm...no...no...no!*

He surely could see through the windows, as he was brought to the front door, the orderlies holding down a man as a blood-spattered surgeon lifted a crimson-stained knife and made a rapid, circular cut around an arm, mangled much like Latimer's own. He certainly heard the pitiful scream as hot steel cut into raw, tender flesh. He undoubtedly saw strange pyramids below each window they carried him past, and in the flickering candlelight realized the unbelievable: They were human limbs discarded recklessly out the windows as just so much unwanted trash. Leaning up against the walls of the house

44

and scattered about the farmyard were the broken bodies of those the surgeon was finished with, and those yet to be taken into the stinking Hell of the front room. He may have even seen Capt. William D. Brown, commander of one of the batteries in Latimer's outfit, lying, suffering from a double amputation performed a few short hours before. As he was taken into the front parlor, he could see that blood was everywhere, in spots and rivulets on the floor. He must have known also, as the kindly bearers brought him through the front door, the surgeon's bloody table was to be his fate as well and that his own blood would soon co-mingle with that already spilled. How a young man, not yet twenty, could have stood the dreadful anticipation is beyond comprehension.

Hopefully, Latimer's time on the operating table was brief. It usually was. Some surgeons prided themselves on the rapidity with which they could cut through the skin and muscle, saw through the bone and sew up veins, arteries, and the flap of skin covering the stump. It was better to get something like that over as quickly as possible. Often, the patient received only a shot or two of army whiskey before the operation to make him giddy if not pain-free. Sometimes, for the officers, the orderlies would save some anesthetic to knock them out. One can only hope young Major Latimer—late VMI cadet—had the benefit of at least that.

Either the wound was too severe or he had lost too much blood spilling to the floor of Mrs. Lady's once lovely parlor floor, or the surgeon's saws carried some then-unknown microbe to be deposited in the young major's body from the last patient, but his life ended not with old age but with his premature death three weeks before his twentieth birthday. The Virginia Military Institute lost another hero to the war.

Carried by loving comrades the scores of miles back to the Old Dominion before he succumbed, Major J. W. Latimer was buried at VMI in far-off Lexington, Virginia. But his legacy may have remained in part in the farmhouse where his sufferings were most grievous, in a corner of the battlefield of Gettysburg.

If young Major Latimer's suffering were the only human agony poured out in the ersatz operating room which was once Mrs. Lady's prim parlor, that would be enough to make angels weep. But there was more.

Captain William D. Brown commanded the Chesapeake Artillery of Maryland, a battery under Latimer's command. Because their battery contained the large 20 pounder Parrott guns, Brown's men were placed on the north side of the Hanover Road, farther away from the enemy. The distance apparently did no good as far as their safety was concerned. Just as the firing was to begin, gallant Captain Brown rode to the front of his battery to deliver a few encouraging words to his men of Maryland. A Yankee solid shot suddenly roared in and passed completely through his horse, hitting Brown's right leg and breaking his left to bits. The fallen horse landed upon him and broke ribs. His men struggled to extract him from under the kicking, dying animal and placed him on a litter. He spoke to some others of the battery as he was carried past, well-aware of his fate, requesting that someone tell his father that he died doing his duty. He also candidly reported that things were not going well on the ridge. They carried him back to Daniel Lady's farmhouse and to Mrs. Lady's hideous parlor. Once inside, the surgeon quickly cut off one pant leg. Looking at his mangled limbs they decided to do what was normally a foregone conclusion: amputate. His service records are painfully succinct: "Both legs fractured. Amputated." Hopefully, Captain Brown was given some laudanum, or at least a shot or two of that army whiskey, before they started cutting; hopefully the surgeon's knife and saw were still relatively sharp, since Brown was wounded early in the fight. Not that whatever "care" the surgeons could provide in Mrs. Lady's parlor-turned-operating room helped. Again the terse notation from his records: "Died July 11, '63."[1]

*   *   *

The Gettysburg Battlefield Preservation Association (GBPA) can trace its roots back to some of the earliest efforts to preserve the fields and land sanctified by the blood of patriots that surround the small town named after one of the first settlers.

The GBPA was founded in 1959 with the specific task of purchasing endangered battlefield tracts for donation or resale to the National Park Service at Gettysburg. President Dwight D. Eisenhower was a proud member of the organization, of which he said, "I am emphatic in my approval of what the GBPA is doing... the battlefield should be preserved as a remembrance of the sacrifice made by men who fought for the things in which they believed." As allied commander of the D-Day Invasion of Normandy, his words ring true across the American generations, from the ghosts in "blue and gray" to their great-grandsons in khaki.

Television pioneer personality "Charlie Weaver" (Cliff Arquette) and other Gettysburg businessmen were instrumental in its beginnings as the first public/private partnership at Gettysburg. After a hiatus of a few months, in 1982, Gettysburg National Military Park Superintendent John Ernst requested that some local historians reconstitute the organization. Famed historian William A. Frassanito, local businessman George Olinger, Gettysburg Borough Preservation Officer Dr. Walter Powell, and Dr. Bruce Bugbee of Gettysburg College were some of the esteemed personages who responded to his challenge.

Over the years the GBPA has saved for posterity the Meals Farm, a huge section of land east of the Mummasburg Road, and the Willoughby Run Tract—sites of the fighting on the first bloody day at Gettysburg. The Wolf, Timbers and Taney Farms, and the Colgrove Tract, scenes of conflict and heartbreak on July 2 were rescued. A tract at East Cavalry Battlefield, where men and their horses, like ancient knights, clashed for supremacy on July 3, was saved. Sachs Bridge, where Union and Confederate soldiers crossed with desperate, rushing, and perhaps final footsteps, was replaced after being literally washed away during winter floods on Marsh Creek with the help of local businesses, government and private donations.

The GBPA even helped honor the dead of all wars by purchasing and razing non-historic buildings adjacent to the Gettysburg National Cemetery Annex at the corner of Steinwehr Avenue and the Taneytown Road and at the Peace Light Memorial. In all, some 2,000 acres of historic land has been saved. No contemporary preservation organization has saved so much hallowed ground.[2]

But perhaps its greatest triumph to date is the purchasing and saving of the Daniel Lady Farm, 140 acres which embrace an historic farmhouse and barn, all once used by Confederate soldiers, surgeons, and officers such as General Robert E. Lee.

While no government marker proclaims the fact, it is the extreme left flank of the Confederate Army of Northern Virginia at Gettysburg. It is where Johnson's Division encamped and built defensive earthworks (remnants of which are still visible) and from where they launched their attack on Culp's Hill and East Cemetery Hill on the evening of July 2, 1863. Johnson's Division's casualties, according to the Official Records, amounted to 229 killed, 1,269 wounded, and 375 missing. The famed Confederate commander Robert E. Lee visited the farm to discuss battle plans and spent several hours of the night of July 1 there. What is truly astounding is that the Lady Farm has remained virtually unspoiled since the battle while entire historic farms along many of the other major roads leading into Gettysburg were gobbled up and leveled for hotels, restaurants and parking lots by corporate conglomerates. But as far as the GBPA is concerned, the Lady Farm will remain a hold-out of historic sanctuary forever.

According to Daniel Lady's claim for damages after the battle, his farm, "...contains 200 acres which was injured by being encamped upon & driven over by the Rebel forces, his buildings were used for hospital purposes, upon the return of the family on Saturday [July 4], wounded soldiers were in the house and dead bodies lying around which they were obliged to bury."

Of course that curt description belies the horrors also embraced by the farmlands, the barn and the ancient house. And it speaks not at all to the unexplainable events that have occurred there.

Late in 2000, I received a letter from a reenactor who portrays a member of Cooper's Battery B, ironically, one of the Union batteries that wreaked so much destruction upon Latimer's men and horses, and some of the infantrymen of Johnson's Division who occupied the fields behind the Lady Farm.

He wrote of an encampment they had on the Lady Farm in October of that year. On Saturday afternoon they explored the fields across which the Confederates had advanced to attack the Union lines on Culp's and Cemetery

Hills. Later that night around the campfire, five of them decided to explore a little farther to the old Confederate lines across the field. It was midnight. They'd gotten about halfway across the darkened field. Suddenly, one of the men asked them to stand still and be quiet. To their utter amazement, as the sound of their shuffling through the high grass ceased, it was replaced by another, more puzzling sound. As the writer stated: "...you could hear sounds all around us. Not natural sounds. There is a certain sound that the tin cups we use make when they bang against our haversacks. None of us had haversacks on but that sound could be heard around us. All of us could hear it, plain as anything."

Cautiously, listening to the sounds of a phantom army on the march, like attacking infantry of another era, they pressed on towards the tree line that marked the former Confederate campsite. "As soon as we entered the woods, all sounds stopped. I mean all sounds. The cups rattling, the crickets and the breeze that was blowing. Every hair on my body stood up. There was a sudden feeling of someone...watching and waiting. We were all very frightened but we were still going to try to go on. We all took one step, and that was it. There was no way any of us could go any farther."

Were the old battlelines manned again? Was there a phantom division again in the position it held fourteen decades before, called into action by some ancient vow to a country now non-existent? Were their eyes once more aglow with the fire of mortal combat? Were their spirit-senses piqued as of old, warriors again beckoned from some unknown, dark land to fight... and die once more?

He mentioned that, while they adhered to the ancient boast that "artillery never retreats," he did admit that they made a spirited "advance to the rear," crossing the three-quarters of a mile back to camp in record time.

True to all reenactors, while camping on the Lady Farm they were in their blue Union artillerist's uniforms. "While we were in the field," he wrote of the phantom army dug in along Mr. Lady's ridgeline, "they didn't seem to really mind, but they were not going to let us actually enter their camp."

Travelers on the Hanover Road notice that each time they pass the Lady Farm, something is mysteriously missing or changed: A pile of brush which, for years has lain dormant, has vanished; a huge board from the side of the barn is missing—the next day it is replaced; someone, apparently in the dead of night, has been altering the pointing in the stonework; the front porch appears as if it has collapsed and the following day the rubble has seemingly de-materialized, leaving the front of the house looking as it did when Confederate soldiers occupied it.

I can solve those mysteries right now.

In the last several years, many volunteers from the Gettysburg Battlefield Preservation Association have put countless hours of time, energy, and their own money into the stabilization and restoration of the Daniel Lady house, barn and farm. Interestingly enough, the GBPA doesn't have a single paid person on staff. Unlike some non-profits where 95% of every donation goes to "administrative costs," (like the Executive Director's salary), everything at the GBPA done by volunteers.

And from those loyal preservationists who have worked on the Daniel Lady Farm come several stories of strange sightings and weird apparitional noises. It is a known fact that any change in the physical status quo of an historic structure seems to animate its resident spirits. So it was that the first winter of physical renovation of the Lady farmhouse was also the resident spirits' winter of their discontent.

Craig Caba, one-time president of the GBPA has probably spent hundreds upon hundreds of hours doing physical labor at the farm—from re-pointing the stone foundation of the barn, to plastering, to woodwork—and therefore has had numerous rare opportunities to witness any manifestations of the unquiet dead.

He recalls working late one night and hearing, from the unoccupied upper floors, the dinging of a small bell. Investigation proved there was no instrument capable of such a noise anywhere in the house. Nor was there anyone to cause any such noise. Yet there it came again, a faint, but distinct, "ding...ding... ding..." like a latter-day death knell for the men and boys of the late Confederate States of America, who gave up the ghost in the confines of farmer Lady's home.

He was laboring there late on another night with two other workers. The two women were painting the front window frames blue in Mrs. Lady's parlor, the scene of unbearable pain and abject horror to scores of Southern wounded. He was on the other side of the wall in the hallway into which the front door opens. There is a full glass storm door on the outside.

Suddenly his eye was caught by something "whisping" past the glass door, "like snow blowing by,"...except that it wasn't snowing. At first he thought it was his own reflection, and so waved a hand to confirm it. But his hand did not appear in the glass. He had to step out from the wall and re-adjust his angle to the door before he could see himself.

Shortly afterwards, the two women came out into the hallway, "with white faces and wide eyed." Without knowing what Craig had seen just ten minutes earlier, they reported that they had seen whispy, white forms pass outside of the two front windows as they were painting them.

So what were these white, amorphous shapes that moved in the footsteps of the weary soldiers carrying wounded comrades to the door of the Lady's farmhouse—136 years after the fact? Some say that, if human remorse is not reconciled or an act of mercy not fulfilled, it is destined to be acted out again and again and again for all eternity. The kind-hearted litter bearers who carried the sufferers into that house hoped with all their might that they would be allowed to carry them back out again, repaired by the surgeons, to return home and suffer no more. In so many cases, it was not meant to be. And so, do the kindly, good-hearted litter-bearers at the Lady Farm suffer torment as well, in search of redemption for their acts of attempted kindness gone unrealized?

And while it is one thing to research and write about unexplainable events that happen to others, it is quite another to experience one myself. In over thirty years of living in Gettysburg (and another dozen or so of previously visiting as a "tourist,") I have had only a few personal journeys deep into the land of the paranormal. The one that occurred in the spring of 2001, at the Daniel Lady Farm was indeed one of the most bizarre and troubling of all.

It was about 11:00 A.M. on Friday, April 27, 2001. I had returned from an errand and saw that I had a message on my answering machine. It was from the caretaker of the farmhouse where Major Latimer, Captain Brown and so many other brave young men suffered and died for their doomed cause.

"Mark," said his voice on the machine, "if you want to see a paranormal event happening right before your eyes, you'd better get out to the farm right now."

That was all. I tried to call back to get more information, but no one answered. I grabbed my camcorder and digital camera and drove out to the farm. On the way I began to have second thoughts. Although I've written and researched hundreds of stories and have read hundreds more sent to me, I was apparently driving right into one that was occurring at this moment. What was I going to see when I got there? Ectoplasm rising from scores of graves that once surrounded the house? Objects in a room flying about, launched by some unseen, angry hands? Spirits careening about the grounds where humans did their very best to drive themselves into extinction? The ultimate chaos before the fabled Final Judgment, begun here, on the battlefield where Northern Cains slew Southern Abels? The End of the World must start somewhere, and the site of a 19th Century Armageddon is as likely a place as any.

But perhaps even more ominously, as I pulled into the driveway, the place looked deserted. I anxiously walked to the front door feeling that someone was watching. I knocked on the door but no one answered. I began to go around the house to knock on the back door when the man who had called me met me in the yard.

"What's going on?" I said, trying not to sound apprehensive.

"Come on," he said, and led me into the front door.

He gave me the background of events during the last weekend.

Volunteers from the Gettysburg Battlefield Preservation Association had been at the farm doing some much-needed repairs: electrical work and particularly some plaster patching and sanding. It took a while to clean everything up, but it was done after the work was finished, mainly because the farm was to have some visitors.

There had been reenactors at the farm and he had given them basic historical information on the farm and house.

He had discovered, while living there, a piece of iron shell imbedded deeply into a solid oak rafter. It was next to the stone wall of the barn, showing evidence of cannon damage, obviously blown out by a misdirected artillery shell. Inside the house, he showed them the restored and, since the repair work, freshly cleaned front room—Mrs. Lady's parlor—which he had furnished with a surgeons' kit so that the reality of the cold steel saw and lancet and scalpel would leave nothing to the imagination as to what happened within the walls of the room.

Imagine the unquiet souls floating about that once horrid room, reliving their former bodies' agonies as bits and pieces of them were hacked off and their life's blood drained from them. Some believe that they can see us from the Other World just as we, occasionally, see them from this world. Do they wonder about reenactors—those they see dressed as they were dressed when they last strode this solid earth? Are the dead curious about those they know they will soon meet as we wonder how we can postpone that inevitable meeting as long as possible, all of us, sooner or later, becoming "beggars before the door of God"?

Finally, he showed the reenactors—who were dressed in the same type of uniform that was, when in this room, torn and bloodied—an actual bloodstain, oval, about a foot in diameter, to the side of the room near a wall. As well, he showed them the bloody hand-print—four fingers and a thumb—against one wall near the door, of a man lifting himself, perhaps to be next upon the surgeon's butcher block. In spite of 138 years of scrubbing with harsh lye soap by Mrs. Lady and the various housewives after her, the bloodstains remained emblazoned, a signature of some men's—perhaps Major Latimer or Captain Brown's—unendurable suffering as their very life's blood pooled below them.

"Where's the paranormal event occurring?" I asked.

He pointed to the door of the parlor.

"What should I look for," I asked, not knowing if something was going to fly at me or confuse my eardrums with some strange noise whose source I could not detect.

His answer did not comfort me: "You'll know it when you see it."

As we entered the small room, I looked around, concentrating on the walls and the ceiling, since that is where much "orb activity" is photographed. It was when I looked down to take careful steps that I saw it.

In the center of the room, where the operating table must have stood, there was a dark, rust-colored liquid, flowing from apparently eighteen to twenty large, dark spots. Some of the liquid streams had flowed into one another, making even larger splotches. The liquid had flowed from the main area of stains toward the fireplace. (In many older houses the floor is pulled downward by the settling of the fireplace.) Alongside the "flow" there appeared to be a clear, watery substance that had separated out, like serum. The droplets were very dark rust-color and within them some of the liquid appeared to have crystallized into a crust. Some of the serum and drops were still wet.

"Is that what I think it is?" I asked.

"I don't know. What do you think it is?"

I didn't want to commit, but the more I looked, the more I realized that it could only be one thing. "I'm not sure I want to say."

I took out my camcorder and recorded the scene. He said that he didn't want to be shown in any of the videos or pictures. Respecting his wishes, I kept the video camera pointed away from him when it was running, but his words and the story of the unbelievable discovery were recorded.

We located a yardstick and laid it beside the stains as a reference. I finished taping and began taking still photos. I even took pictures of the white ceiling, thinking that maybe a leak from upstairs had caused the floorboards to yield up some of the ancient stain once applied for decoration. But there was no evidence on the ceiling of a leak; the tape shows that clearly.

Stains on Daniel Lady Farm Floor

I was curious as to what the substance might really be. I got some tissue and dipped it into one of the spots that already looked as if it had started to crystallize. It wicked up the rust-colored fluid and seemed to dry immediately on the tissue. I placed it in a secure pocket of my camera case. Then he took me on a tour of the rest of the house and told me some of his other encounters with the supernatural in this house that had the misfortune to be built on the site where one of the bloodiest battlefields in human history would someday be located.

He told me that he had been hearing strange noises from the time he moved in, especially coming from that front parlor. He and members of the GBPA who had been working at the farm heard, at separate times, jingling sounds coming from that front room as well as what he described as "mumbling."

I visited the parlor one more time before I left the farmhouse, trying to reconcile the long, gory trails along the floor. I could not.

The caretaker said that he had work to do in the fields and headed out. I left the farmhouse at about 1:00 P.M. I returned to the Ghosts of Gettysburg Tour Headquarters and finished whatever errands I had. At about 4:00 P.M., Carol, my then fiancé, answered the phone and took a message. It was the caretaker of the farm again. He needed me to return immediately.

Once again I packed all my gear and headed out to the Lady Farm. I entered the hallway and was greeted by the caretaker who had just come in from working in the field. He was obviously more agitated than just a few hours before. The first thing he did was apologize.

"If you smell alcohol on my breath, I'm sorry. I needed a couple shots to calm my nerves."

He pointed to the closed door of the parlor and I took his lead. Slowly, I opened the old door to the room that once contained human agony to overflowing. Again I had the apprehensive feeling as to what might assault my senses upon entering. I walked through the door carefully and moved cautiously toward the fireplace trying not to step on the damp, dark stains. There was only one problem.

The stains were gone.

I stood gaping at the floor. I looked at the caretaker, who stood with a puzzled look on his face.

"What..." I stuttered. "Where did...how?"

He shrugged his shoulders and shook his head.

There was not a trace of liquid on the floor where, just three hours before, the unmistakable trail of what appeared to be the body's life fluid was promiscuously spilled.

"After you left I did some work outside," he said. "I came back and this is what I saw. It was right here, wasn't it? In the video, you can see him squat down where the rust-colored stains once soaked the floor and sweep his hand along it. "What the heck?...Look at this dust." Not only was the floor bone dry, but coated in a dust so fine you could barely see it on his fingertips. I looked around: across the entire floor was a virtually invisible, thin coating of fine, powder-like dust. It was laid down so evenly as to make one believe that it had taken weeks of settling to produce such a delicate, thin layer.

It was almost as if I had been in a time-warp. The floor with its thin layer of dust should have been there first, then the liquid stains laid down over it. But the video tape and its built-in time-stamp are unmistakable as to the chronology: the stains came first, then their disappearance, then the thin coating of dust, all within two or three hours.

But the most bizarre, alarming thing was yet to be.

Carol remembered the sample in my camera case in the vehicle. She ran out to see if it too had disappeared. If several wide swaths of dark red liquid mysteriously vanished, what had become of the sample I had taken away?

I opened the case and gently lifted the tissue out. There it was, a reddish-brown stain with fading, ragged edges, like serum had separated from it.

Some members of the GBPA are well-connected. The stained tissue was sent to one of the most prestigious crime labs in the country for testing. Three weeks later, the results came back.

The mysterious substance was, indeed, blood.

There was only one more question to reluctantly ask: what species was it?

Again the answer that defies all logic.

The blood was human.

Why, if the horror had been so acute and the pain so great, would the spirit want to return to the site of its body's most traumatic experience? What uncommon, unearthly logic would compel the spiritual vestige of a life to revisit the place where it was cast off to forever roam the world in search of peace and rest? And why is no rest granted and the shadow of a life forced to manifest itself in unexplainable, relentless, strange ways like bloodstains that appear...then vanish?

THE BRIDGE OF SIGHS

I stood...on the Bridge of Sighs,
A palace and a prison on each hand.

–Lord Byron

In art and literature, through myth and life, bridges can be more symbolic than real. They represent a passage and safe return; but they also represent the possibility of no return. In war their practical and symbolic stature grows.

The symbol of the bridge is so great that chroniclers of war cannot help but use it: *The Bridge over the River Kwai*; *The Bridges at Toko Ri*; Emerson's "rude bridge that arched the flood" at Concord. Beyond the poet, the historian can list bridges that mattered in war: The Stone Bridge at First Manassas; Burnside's Bridge at Antietam; The pontoon bridges at Fredericksburg; Pegasus Bridge on D-Day; The Bridge at Remagen over the Rhine.

Sachs Bridge Photo Courtesy of Darlene Perrone

There is a quaint bridge just outside of Gettysburg named after the family that owned the property upon which it stands. Sachs Bridge witnessed a great deal during the battle-torn days of July 1-3, 1863.[1]

Both Union and Confederate troops used the span to maneuver. Union troops crossed the bridge during the first day's fighting, before the area became part of the Confederate rear, then after the battle to scout and pursue the rebels as they retreated. Since Confederates encamped in the vicinity and set up field hospitals for the hundreds of wounded trickling back from the savage fighting on July 2, arriving Union soldiers saw the results of the fighting in The Peach Orchard, The Wheatfield, Devil's Den, Little Round Top: wounded Confederates who were unable to be evacuated; burials of those who had already been evacuated to the Higher Plane. They were buried out of the way, in a place where they could easily have been forgotten. Some historians have estimated that anywhere from 800 to 1,300 soldiers from both sides continue to endure a not-so-peaceful rest under the sod at Gettysburg, unknown, unfound, and saddest of all, un-mourned. If the historians are correct, a good many of those could remain around Sachs Bridge.

There is a rumor that, during the battle, three Confederate deserters were executed by hanging from the rafters of the bridge. There is, however, no historical evidence that Robert E. Lee, or any Southern commander ordered an execution of any soldiers during the battle. Something like that would have to be recorded somewhere, and it is not. Besides, Death was accomplishing his own executions, by the thousands, within sight of the bridge using God's own children dressed in blue and gray as his executioners. Still, there are the sightings of ghostly mists swinging and twisting, seemingly suspended from the crossbeams of the old bridge....

My own experiences at the bridge go back to the days when I was first introduced to the techniques of paranormal investigating by Rick Fisher, one of the pioneers in the art of "ghost hunting." Rick had been the first one to approach me after the first *Ghosts of Gettysburg* book came out to explain the weird "orbs," "vortexes," and "ectoplasm" he had been photographing at cemeteries and on the battlefield. He helped me, with the aid of his remote thermal scanner, to locate and photograph my first ectoplasm (some like to call it "paranormal mist") at the Point of Woods, long rumored to be haunted, where Pickett's men launched themselves into oblivion. He had been out to Sachs Bridge a month or so before and had found it particularly active and invited me to go along on a second trip. Upon arrival I realized how dark and secluded the area can be.

The waters of Marsh Creek pass opaquely, silently below, hiding who-knows-what beneath their still surface. A dark path worn by generations of fishermen, or perhaps a remnant of the thousands of trips by hospital orderlies to gather water for the wounded, leads off into a darker wood beside the creek.

One rumor has a figure with a lantern on that path beckoning visitors deeper into the sinister woods. The fields to the west of the bridge are open, but in the claustrophobic darkness, seem impossibly peopled. It's just a feeling that someone, out there in the dark, is watching your soul.

There were a few other investigators at the bridge the night Rick took me there. Some left and the bridge was practically deserted. Rick handed me an infra-red night-vision scope—the kind modern soldiers use to detect an enemy in total darkness—and told me to look through it down the bridge. I leaned against one of the short pillars used for blocking vehicular traffic and did as he told me. I wasn't sure what to expect.

A minute went by. Then two. Frankly, I was getting bored.

"Uh, Rick. What should I be looking for?"

His response was cryptic: "You'll know it when you see it."

Another twenty seconds passed. Then, like a startling, sudden, inscrutable enigma, it was there...then it was gone!

A bright orb that appeared to be the size of a baseball, came through the roof of the bridge, centered itself in my night vision scope as if curious as to what order of being I was, then did a ninety-degree turn and flew out of the bridge to the left at an impossible rate of speed.

I can't recall exactly what I said—no doubt it was an expletive—and turned to Rick who was smiling. I was stunned. As they say, you could have knocked me over with a feather.

I had seen still photos of "orbs," but this was the first time I'd seen one in motion, "live," if that is what you can call what is supposed to be the spirit of the dead. It was not an insect or animal because it was a perfect sphere and had no wings or legs or body. It was bright (green, since it was seen through the night vision scope), and it paused as if exercising curiosity at my presence. And when it made the ninety-degree turn to my left, it accelerated from almost a dead stop, and sped off faster than a tracer bullet.

My second personal experience at Sachs Bridge came on a Halloween morning just before dawn. Jim Cooke was a deejay for a local station and was doing his annual "Ghosts of Gettysburg" live radio show. Several people were out at the bridge, including famed psychic Karyol Kirkpatrick. We had crossed to the far side of the bridge. Karyol suddenly stopped. We asked her if she wanted to go into the woods on the far side of the bridge, and, for the first time ever in an investigation, I heard her say no. She left the bridge immediately.[2]

Another investigator was standing next to me at that end of the bridge looking through a night vision scope I had purchased after my incredible experience with Rick. For some reason—intuition, perhaps—I turned my camera up and shot a quick random picture into the rafters of the bridge.

At virtually the same moment, the investigator with the night vision scope exclaimed, "Hey, I think I see something!" As well, in the small monitor in the back of the camera I had seen a brief glimpse of some amorphous light, the image of which, because of the nature of the camera I was using, had quickly disappeared.

"I got something too," I said and activated the photo replay setting.

There, floating through the rafters, seemingly with its arms outstretched, was ectoplasm, in the classic ghost pose, flying through the air. I showed it to the other investigator.

"That's exactly what I saw," she said excitedly, "passing through the night vision scope!" A mutual sighting at Sachs Bridge was confirmed and recorded.

Another group of investigators visited the bridge in March 1999.[3] They had set up a video camera with the "night vision" feature on a tripod in the middle of the bridge. They had been there about 30 minutes and were getting no results. At the far end of the bridge were some college students who had come out to the bridge to drink beer and get scared. They got what they wanted. As did the investigators.

The taping had just begun when the students leapt from their place at the end of the bridge and ran, obviously terrified, toward the camcorder. The cameraman, looking through his viewfinder, began shouting that "they" were coming right at the group. The woman who related the story began snapping pictures in the direction the camcorder was pointed.

They finally got the students to stop (except for one poor young lady who ran right to their car and refused to come out!) and asked them what had happened. They replied almost in unison that, while sitting peacefully at the far end of the bridge, they suddenly all saw a huge and menacing shadow loom up before them, and heard what they identified as the sound of hooves coming towards them and running past them as they tried to escape.

The investigators rewound the tape. There, on the tape, emerging from the darkened end of the bridge, could be seen the students, panic-stricken, running as if for their lives towards and past the camcorder. There, seemingly in pursuit, some eight orbs were flying right behind them as the students tried in vain to escape the sound of pounding hooves.

The investigators decided to attempt to recreate the scene. As inactive as the bridge was for the thirty minutes before, suddenly it became a hotbed of activity. Five times they ran towards the camcorder and five times a squadron of orbs pursued them to their destination.

When they returned home, they replayed the tape on their large screen television. With a larger picture and more detail they saw that the orbs actually had tails, "like a comet," one investigator wrote.

The bridge has also proved to be a laboratory for studying EVP—electronic voice phenomena: the alleged voices of the dead—from the reports of those who have studied the experiences there of people who cannot hear.

A researcher in infra-red photography from Pittsburgh related the following story from Sachs Bridge.

His wife is deaf, as are her two friends. It was afternoon. They were visiting the bridge, but were aware of the paranormal aspects of the site. He was taking pictures when his wife suddenly indicated that she was having a paranormal experience. He took her picture and an orb appeared near her ear. He asked her what she had experienced. She said she heard voices. The other fellow was at the far end of the bridge. Suddenly he ran back to the group, obviously frightened. Asked what happened, he told them that he heard someone talking at that end of the bridge, when there was no one there.

In May 2006, another paranormal investigator was visiting Sachs Bridge with her hearing impaired friend. She said that without his hearing aids he is nearly deaf. There were many other investigators at the bridge that night. It was approaching midnight. (Since her writing, Sachs Bridge has been closed after dark. The bridge is an historic treasure and some evidence of ritual candle-burning *on the wooden bridge* indicated a dangerous mis-use of the site.)

Her friend, Shawn, began acting strangely almost immediately after they arrived, evincing strong concentration and wandering off by himself. When the female investigator approached him he asked her to take a photo of him; a faint orb appeared near his right shoulder at ear-level. He told her to continue snapping photos; in every one she took, an orb hovered near. Later, he said that he had been "hearing something" in his hearing aids, but he couldn't explain exactly what it was except to liken it to the sound of electricity. Further analysis of her photos showed that in nearly every one he was looking in the direction of the orb.

She mentioned that Shawn became even more intense—more intense than she had ever seen him in the years they'd know each other. He didn't move for several minutes. She likened his concentration to a trance. When he finally came out of it, he mentioned that he had been hearing a voice, either female or that of a boy or possibly a young soldier. Unfortunately, he couldn't make out what the voice was saying.

As an experiment, Shawn removed his hearing aids. Photos show that he was still attracting orbs. Later, he said that he was still hearing the same phenomena!

They were standing near the west entrance to the bridge. Suddenly they looked at each other and simultaneously asked, "Did you hear that?" Shawn heard the sharp report of a gunshot; she heard a man cry out in agony. Her take on it: "I'm guessing what happened was we each heard the same paranormal event, but he heard the gun fire, and I heard the yell of the man who had the sorrowful misfortune of receiving that devastating blow from a musket fired 143 years ago."

There is the path that leads along Marsh Creek on the west side of the bridge. Shawn was drawn to it. Investigators from other groups, realizing that he seemed to be acting as a paranormal "magnet" began to follow him.

Remember now, it was well past midnight. The area around Sachs Bridge needs no ghost stories to be frightening; the real stories of the site are scary enough. As well as being used as a staging area for Confederate assaults during the battle, it became filled with temporary field hospitals with men writhing in agony beneath the surgeons' rapidly dulling bone saws. Often the surgeons were not successful in saving the horribly wounded. The area near the bridge then became a graveyard. Though exhumation parties eventually plucked rotted bodies from the soil around Sachs Bridge, being Confederates, they had lain in un-consecrated, uneasy sepulture for years after the battle. Who knows if the parties got them all? Walking that pathway where so many wounded and dying struggled to get to the waters of Marsh Creek, where others may still be entombed, during the daylight is enough to send a chill down your spine. At night, when all the senses are limited, the horror is magnified....

The two investigators and their impromptu entourage made their way down the path. After a few minutes he turned his head to the right and said, "What?" and asked that his friend take a picture. He looked at the LCD screen and said, "Thank you! Thank you very much!" He explained that he'd heard a voice beckon, "Over here!" When she looked at the screen she saw a large orb seemingly attached to the tree at a height of about 6 feet. As any good investigator would, she took several more photos, and the orb remained attached to the tree, indicating to her that it was paranormal and not dust too close to the lens.

Other sounds were heard, including a sharp knocking on the bridge. The investigator heard a booming voice call out, "Virginia!" In spite of the fact that there were numerous people at the site, no one else heard the battle cry from beyond.

Finally, as they were walking back to the bridge, Shawn stopped in his tracks, turned to his right and asked, "What did you say?" The other investigator, having learned her lesson, instinctively snapped a picture in that direction. She asked Shawn what he'd heard. He replied that he'd heard a voice say, "Get out!" They decided that they would respect the unearthly request and leave the area. Looking at the photo she'd just took, she saw a "medium-sized, reddish, orb-like mass" hovering in a nearby tree.

So the mysteries still remain: Just how do we know the Other World? Apparently instruments and technology can take us only so far into that vast land just over Reality's horizon. Human senses (and ultra-senses) evidently are the key. We are a vital component in the link with the dead. That there is something there seems without doubt. How we tap into what must be the ultimate knowledge is now the challenge.

TALES FROM THE GUIDES

But that the dread of something after death,
The undiscovered country, from whose bourn
No traveler returns, puzzles the will,
And makes us rather bear those ills we have,
Than fly to others that we know not of....
—William Shakespeare, *Hamlet, Act. 3, Scene i.*

Scattered throughout the books in my *Ghosts of Gettysburg* series are random stories told to me by people who should, by all rights, be jaded by sightings of wispy spirits or strange noises reminiscent of past events echoing through darkened streets, or odd, ancient smells wafting across fields upon which once decomposed the tattered human debris left by the great battle in Gettysburg. Since 1994, the guides from the Ghosts of Gettysburg Candlelight Walking Tours® night after night, have gone to the very edge of Reality's horizon taking our customers with them. Occasionally, (actually more frequently than one would suppose) they and our unwary customers are treated to an event that is so out of the ordinary, it can only be classified as paranormal. I hear more bizarre stories each year.

These stories come not from new guides prone to hysterical assumptions about the slightest rustling in the street. Barbara[1] is one of our more experienced guides having been with the company over six years. Her route takes her past the Gettysburg Borough Building, formerly the Adams County Library and, during the time of the battle, the county jail. It is closed for business at the time our tours pass it. One night, she began telling the story of "Gus," an inmate or former cook at the jail who, while the building was the library, rode the empty elevator up and down, got a drink from the water fountains, and filled the building at opening time with the smells of fresh breakfast being cooked. All of these while remaining invisible, of course.

For a while, the Borough had electric candles burning in each window of the building. Standing across the street, Barbara told the story of Gus. When she finished, one of her customers asked her if she had seen the candle in the window. "What candle?" she asked since all the windows had candles in them. Several others on the tour piped up and told her that when she began the story of Gus, a candle in a second floor window extinguished, and when she finished, it went back on again.

Fast-forward one year: Barbara was again at the Borough Building, which, by then, had all the candles removed from the windows. She told the story about Gus extinguishing and re-lighting the candle and joked about how Gus, since he had no candles to manipulate, now had to make a personal appearance. One of the several people who were taking pictures suddenly said, "Hey, I got a face in my picture!" Barbara looked at the back of the camera and confirmed the image of a human face peering out from a window in the building. Which window? The same one on the second floor where they saw the candle extinguish, then re-light just a year before.

Of all the anachronisms war brings, none is more acutely painful to the human heart as what is done on sanctified ground. The American Civil War was no exception, for you have soul rending battles swirling like evil dervishes around places like Shiloh Church in Tennessee, or the Dunkard Church at Antietam, Maryland, or St. George's Episcopal Church in Fredericksburg, Virginia. The fighting at Gettysburg was also no exception to this desecration. Local churches filled to the brim with torn, bleeding bodies and surgeons about to make them bleed more. A Union chaplain, leaving the Lutheran Church on Chambersburg Street, after nurturing the worried souls of the wounded inside, was shot dead on the step by a Confederate standing in the street; the hallowed floor of the German Reformed Church on Stratton Street was drilled full of holes to let the life's blood of hundreds of soldiers to drain into the cellar and allow the surgeons to work without slipping. Worst of all, the Lutheran Theological Seminary was not just battlefield, but its buildings blood spattered hospitals, its grounds pitted graveyards, a place where even God couldn't watch.

Barbara also conducts the Seminary Ridge Tour. One of the more magnificent buildings along the tour route is the Rev. Samuel Schmucker house. She informs her tour that the large, Victorian-style house was built in 1833 and is named after the Rev. Samuel Simon Schmucker, the first president of the Lutheran Theological Seminary at Gettysburg. She mentions that the house is used for faculty offices and conferences. It is no longer occupied by a family and is virtually never used in the late evening hours when the tours are conducted. Barbara was walking her group around to the side of the building to show them an artillery shell lodged in the wall since the time of the battle. On the third floor on the front of the building are two dormer windows. One had an air conditioner placed in it. Several people on her tour saw something strange. Although Barbara assured them the house was unoccupied, they claimed they saw a candle in one of the dormer windows. Barbara went back to look, but there was nothing there. She stopped her tour so they could see the artillery shell—a remnant from the savagely violent battle—still embedded in the side of the building. As she looked up at the building she, along with the rest of the tour, realized that there was now a candle in one of the dormer windows on the side of the building, as if the candle had moved from the front to the side dormer. Barbara saw the candle as well, but, skeptic that she is, thought the candle had been in the window all along, but she had never noticed it before. The only problem is that, during the rest of her season as a guide on Seminary Ridge, she made it a point to look and never saw the candle in that window again.

Schmucker House

One night more recently, Barbara was finishing up her tour of Seminary Ridge and was walking her group down the east slope of the Ridge down the walk from "Old Dorm" to Hay Street. She likes that path because it is "darker and creepier under the trees there." Darker and creepier indeed, and if what some members of her tour saw is evidence, more haunted as well. The group was dispersing and a couple approached her and asked her if she had seen the man that was behind the tree at her back. She replied that she was busy telling her story and watching her group's reactions. They said they distinctly saw a man in a soldier's uniform step out from behind the tree to observe the people on the tour. As soon as Barbara had finished her last story, the couple went over to the tree to find the soldier, but he was gone, and they never saw him leave.

Barbara is not the only guide who has experienced the paranormal on our tours. Devon[2] is also a guide who has been with us a number of years. It was the last tour of the 2007 season. Just across Breckenridge Street from the Ghosts of Gettysburg Tour Headquarters is the Tillie Pierce House Bed & Breakfast. Matilda "Tillie" Pierce was a fifteen-year-old Gettysburg girl during the time of the battle whose father had a butcher shop on the corner of Baltimore and Breckenridge Street. On the morning of July 1, 1863, Union soldiers marched by to meet the Confederates north and west of the town. By early afternoon, the townsfolk realized that things were not going well for the Federal army. To be safe, Tillie's next-door neighbor, Mrs. Shriver, was leaving with her small children for her parents' home on the Taneytown Road, south of town, and offered to take Tillie. About 1:00 P.M., they began their walk out the Taneytown Road to the Weikert family's stone farmhouse where they felt certain they would be sheltered from the battle. Unfortunately, she had gone from the proverbial frying pan into the fire: the Weikert farm was directly behind Little Round Top, which was to become one of the bloodiest battle sites on the Gettysburg Battlefield. The next day, wounded Federal soldiers streamed back to the Weikert farmhouse and Tillie's tender age was forgotten. She was thrust into the role as nurse for the scores of torn Union soldiers at the house. After the war, Tillie wrote about her experiences.

The Tillie Pierce House

The Tillie Pierce House was a Gettysburg treasure that had sadly fallen into disrepair. Even a non-profit could not save it. Eventually a couple purchased the Tillie Pierce House and began the process of converting it into a Bed & Breakfast. It was an arduous task: old houses are difficult to restore faithfully to include a modern, money-making business. The best part is that they managed to restore the house without removing its ghosts. Devon's experience is evidence of that.

She had parked across Baltimore Street from the Tillie Pierce House. She had watched them working on the house all summer and noticed that, for the first time, the boards that had covered the windows for a long time, had finally been removed. The restored second floor window sashes were hung, but there were no bottom sashes yet.

It seems to be a given that historic houses, when in the process of being restored or renovated, become more paranormally active. Herr Tavern, the James Gettys Hotel, The Cashtown Inn, even our own Ghosts of Gettysburg Tour Headquarters, had more ghostly activity than before the construction work began. Skeptics will say, "it is the house settling" (strange, since most of the houses have been "settled" since well before the Battle of Gettysburg). Paranormalists, on the other hand, will say it's the former owners or residents rebelling against the change in the physical status quo to which they've become accustomed during the long years of their deaths....

Photo Courtesy of Jeff Ritzmann

While Devon was waiting to start her tour, a woman who had been anxious to take one of our tours all season, approached her and began to tell Devon of her own paranormal experiences. She had been through the Ghosts of Gettysburg Headquarters and asked Devon if we had the ghost of a little boy residing in our building. Devon answered that indeed we do, and the woman proceeded to describe him exactly as several of our mediums who have seen him have. She also said she saw him in the back room. (Interestingly, a paranormal investigator who had spent the night in our building took a remarkable picture in that back room. There, standing in suspendered pants and a white shirt is the shadowy figure of what appears to be a small boy.)

Devon had begun her tour and was walking to her next stop when the same lady approached her and asked her to turn around and look at the top window of the Pierce House. As she turned, Devon saw a movement in the window, "a white movement such as you would see if a curtain was blowing in a breeze." She asked the woman what she had seen and she replied that a teenage girl, "a very pretty young girl with her hair in a braided bun had been standing in the window listening" to Devon's talk. The woman said that when Devon got to the part in her talk about all the deaths that occurred during the battle, the girl "put her hand over her heart and bowed her head."

They continued the tour until they ended up across the street from the Pierce House. Suddenly the woman said, "There she is again." This time the entire tour turned and looked at the Pierce House. To everyone's surprise, there, in the upstairs window stood a young girl, wearing a white dress. "She just stood and looked at us," according to Devon's report. "Then as before all we could see was that image of a curtain blowing in the window. For clarification, there were no curtains in the windows."

Devon summed up the experience: "I think it was Tillie and for the first time in a very, very long time, she could finally see out of those windows of her house. She seemed very sad, but in awe of us. I don't know who she thought we were, but I hope I told the story right, when she was listening to me in the courtyard, for I think I must have reminded her of those days in 1863, as she touched her heart and prayed for those soldiers she cared for so tenderly."

This event in 2007, was not the first time Devon had a paranormal experience on one of her tours. In 2004, she and another guide were finishing up their tour at Alumni Park in front of a building known as Twin Sycamores. I had written about Twin Sycamores in one of the other *Ghosts of Gettysburg* books, and they were relating the stories of how a mother and daughter had seen Civil War soldiers in the house at different times. The sightings, of course, were several decades after the last Civil War soldiers had died. The building then became an insurance office, but still the ghostly activity continued: doors would open and close; after hours, footsteps would begin crossing the first floor and when late night workers would check, no one was to be seen. The women who used to work there late at night began getting all their work done by 5:00 P.M.

It was July 6, just a few days after the anniversary of the battle. Devon and George[3], another guide of long-standing, were wrapping up their tours at about 11:00 P.M. A family interrupted Devon's story to point out what they were seeing in the closed building: In the lower center window there was the shadow of a man with a large round hat peeking out of the window. Devon called to George and showed him what she was seeing. He too saw the apparition, which seemed to be looking straight out of the window, then would walk away and peek out the side of the window. Devon sent two young male volunteers across the street to see if perhaps it was a reflection. They called back across the street that it was freezing where they stood. Sure enough, in spite of the fact that it was a warm July evening, when they returned, the boys were cold to the touch. They commented that when you looked into the window, only the room could be seen, but upon stepping back, the ghost would re-appear. Both groups—some 50 people—were across the street by now, peering in the windows.

Devon recalled that when the ghostly soldier was at the window, small blue, white and green lights, "like small Christmas lights," surrounded him. A man in the group took a picture and the image of a soldier with a blue hat, coat, and pants with a stripe down the leg was visible in the screen. Several more pictures were taken. The group then saw the soldier sitting at an invisible table and moving as if he were feeding himself. Then the crowd saw two more soldiers appear before their eyes. One was without a hat and stood leaning against the back wall; the other peered out the window along with the soldier who was eating. The entire episode went on for nearly an hour with the group standing at the fence not more than a few feet from them. As suddenly as it began, the activity stopped.

The astounded tourists began walking back to their cars, some heading back to the Ghosts of Gettysburg Headquarters, perhaps thinking they would be safe from the ghosts once they got back to the building. Except in Gettysburg, you're never quite safe from our ghosts....

From nearly the first day the Ghosts of Gettysburg tour company bought the Civil War Era house on the corner of Baltimore and Breckenridge Streets, strange, unexplainable events have been occurring.[4] Doors have been opened by some unseen helpful hand for workmen repairing the house. Some have speculated it is the ectoplasmic hand of Jacob Heck who owned the carriage trimmer's shop in the oldest section of the building, one laborer helping out another...across death's door. Children have been heard, seen and felt, rattling a restroom doorknob, appearing in the stairway or in a paranormal investigator's photo, pulling on an employee's sweater, or pushing a customer out a door. Communications have been established with a former owner as well as the soldiers from Georgia and Louisiana who once occupied this section of town, building a rubble barricade across Baltimore Street where it hits Breckenridge. They speak freely on digital recorders, resulting in "EVP" or electronic voice phenomena—the voices of the dead recorded. They utilize "ITC" or Instrumental Trans-communication—operating various electronic instruments such as phones or computers to reveal the secrets denied to us by their deaths. But one recent event piqued the curiosity of a veteran guide and frightened an entire tour and their leaders.

On a weekend in late April 2010, Amy[5], our guide with the most years with the company, was leading a group of 8th graders and their chaperones on a tour. Toward the end of the tour, it began to thunderstorm. The group was close enough to the Tour Headquarters that, even though the building was closed, she could use the covered porch for her last few stories. Amy's stories were dramatically punctuated by flashes of lightning. She told the classic story of the Blue Boy of Stevens Hall whose cold blue face is seen by female occupants of the dorm floating outside their window…three stories up! She had finished that story and had just started the story of the elevator in Pennsylvania Hall that took two unwitting college administrators on a trip to a Civil War Hospital in the cellar. The series of e-mails from Amy will explain what happened best:

"We made it through the thunder and lightning storm. Just wondered, who was that STOMPING through the Ghost Office when we were in the courtyard??? Someone who wanted to go home? If it was a ghost—it was a loud insistent ghost. Got the group going!"

Balcony 271 Baltimore Street

The e-mail was referred to me by Katie, our manager, who assured me that when the storm hit and Amy and her group were on the porch, she had locked up the office and set the alarm. I wrote back to Amy, telling her that no one had been inside the house when she had arrived, and asked what it sounded like.

In her return e-mail she admitted that she thought maybe it was an employee trying to scare them into leaving the porch. But whatever it was seemed to be able to appear, vanish and reappear in a different place virtually instantly, stomping its feet persistently:

"At first it sounded like they were in the guide room/kitchen, behind the door, but then the insistent steps seemed to stomp back and forth across the length of the pre-1880 downstairs. As we were all reacting and I wondering what to do, stay or go, the sound changed, as if 'whoever' had very quickly gone upstairs and was now STOMPING rather insistently and very loudly overhead, back and forth, on the balcony. I couldn't see anyone up there, and I didn't hear any doors open. The whole change of position happened so quickly. It sounded like somebody wanted us out of there, that they had enough, we were annoying them, and we had to go. I looked to a couple chaperones and one said simply, 'Let's go.'"

One of the questions employees of the Ghosts of Gettysburg Candlelight Walking Tours® get most frequently from customers is, "Has anyone ever seen a ghost on your tours?" Ask the guides; their answer, most certainly, will be "Yes!"

LIFE'S COUNTERFEIT

The sleeping and the dead
Are but as pictures...
–William Shakespeare, *MacBeth, Act 2, Scene 1.*

The feature film "Gettysburg" ranks as one of the most sweeping and poignant films about war. It captured, by using thousands of reenactors in some of the more realistically enacted scenes ever to appear on screen, the raw emotion of men in mortal conflict in the Victorian age. And a unique age it was for war, with officers presenting compliments before leading hundreds to their deaths into the inferno of mid-19th Century combat, and soldiers refusing to fire upon another whose conspicuous gallantry made him stand out, a normally easy target in battle. Drive around any Civil War battlefield park with the sound track of the movie playing and it will bring tears to your eyes, evoking the superhuman deeds accomplished by men who found themselves raised above the mere mortal in more ways than one.

Filming began in July 1992, and the town of Gettysburg was inundated with Hollywood stars, onlookers, extras, friends of the Hollywood stars, and, of course, visitors to the town who would have taken their vacations here anyway.

The extras, who were reenactors, encamped several miles southwest of Gettysburg in their little dog tents, or, if they were officers, in larger tents. The bare minimum was supplied by the organizers—which is the way the reenactors like it. Straw, water and firewood was about it. There was an open-sided food tent where the extras could get a meal. The organizers supplied transportation to and from the filming sites and into and back from town for a little rest and relaxation when the extras were done for the day.

I wrote about one woman who was volunteering her time and pickup truck to shuttle reenactors to and from town during the evening hours. After dropping a group off in town, she headed back to the encampment site to pick up another group. Traveling through the darkened battlegrounds, she heard a strange tap...tap...tapping coming from the back of the truck. Looking in the rear-view mirror, she saw several soldiers looking dirty and weary, riding in the back. Convinced, after so many trips in and out of town that she had absent-mindedly picked up some reenactors on her way out of town, she shrugged off the images in her mirror. But the more she thought about it, as she sped along toward the campsite, the more she realized that she had not stopped to pick anyone up on her way out…yet, there they were, in her mirror, and there was that incessant tapping. She practically took the turn into the campsite on two wheels and screeched to a halt in front of the guard gate. She leaped from the cab to ask the reenactors how in the world they could have gotten in the truck when she was moving, but the bed was empty. The security guard, by now, was at her side. "Did anyone jump out of my truck as I came through the gate?" She was answered by a quizzical look and the word, "No."

Over ten years later, the stories from the filming of the movie continue to come in.

I recently received a letter through one of our guides at Ghosts of Gettysburg Candlelight Walking Tours® from a friend who drives a motor coach. During the filming her company had contracted to transport the extras to the shooting sites. She spent most of her summer tramping around after the actors and extras—even wore out a pair of boots—following them over the rough Gettysburg terrain. She had literally *carte blanche* to pass in and out of the sets.

One particularly long day, when the reenactors were finished filming at around 8:30 P.M., she parked the bus and proceeded to walk alone through an open field toward the kitchen tent. It was still light enough to see well. As she was walking, she noticed four reenactors to her right. They were close enough for her to notice some details: One wore a dark brown hat with a wide brim; he was speaking in earnest to the other three and facing her as they walked nearby. Suddenly she felt someone approaching rapidly in the open field on her left from behind. He was coming so quickly that she stepped aside as he walked on past, thinking for a moment that he was so close he might bump into her. She politely said good evening, but was ignored as he continued on his mission.

Working with the film crew and extras, she had been struck by how polite everyone was, and so it bothered her that this particular Confederate cavalry "officer" had been so rude. She turned to see the reaction from the four others to her right…and they had vanished. She turned to her left to locate the Confederate, and he too had disappeared. She stopped in her tracks and realized that she was in the middle of a wide open field and had just witnessed the impossible: five beings gone from the face of the Earth—or at least, this earthly plane—in an instant.

Somewhat in a daze, she stood there for a second, then moved on to the food tent where she sat facing the open field where she had just witnessed the dematerialization of five apparently solid individuals, wondering where they went and why did she not feel the Confederate officer bump into her. She never realized what really had happened until the next summer when she was driving a busload of passengers from the Carlisle Army War College to the Gettysburg Battlefield and their guide started to tell a ghost story about Gettysburg.

Suddenly she realized what she had witnessed. Confusing as their disappearance was, they first appeared so real that, at the time, she never considered the possibility that she had, rather inadvertently, and temporarily, walked into that vague, shadowy land we are all destined someday to inhabit permanently.

THE GHOST TRAIN

Science, ancient Sister of Magick, has begun to realize the human potential that resides, inconspicuously, in the spiral-mapped matter of the brain. Just as the magicians, accused of trafficking with the Devil, were said to have developed tremendous power of natural phenomena, Science has ascended to that realm unblamed, and guiltless.
–From the Introduction to the *Necronomicon*

During the Civil War Period, railroads were the glamour queens of transportation in America. There was nothing like the ease and excitement of riding a train to distant, exotic places across the country as compared to a dusty, bouncing ride in a stagecoach. With speeds topping 20 miles per hour, the rides were breathtaking. Trains carried hundreds of passengers and tons of freight, shrinking travel time and opening up new worlds of commerce for the distant edges of the continent. When civil war came to America, the opposing sides learned the strategic importance of the rail lines.

At the first major battle at Manassas in July 1861, Confederate troops were loaded onto rail cars and transported to the battlefield miles from their encampment. They arrived much more quickly than if they had marched. And, more importantly, they arrived fresh for the fight on the battlefield. It was the first time in history the railroads were used to fight a battle.

In subsequent battles and campaigns, the railroads played an important role, moving not only troops and arms, but horses and large guns, food and ammunition, and the wounded to the rear. Cutting the rail lines supplying Petersburg, Virginia, became the aim of U. S. Grant in one of the final campaigns of the war. The siege took nine months, primarily because the Confederates also knew that cutting the rail lines would sever their supply lines, rendering Petersburg and their capital Richmond untenable.

Destroying the rail lines in the south was a major objective of Sherman during his march through Georgia and the Carolinas. The peculiar way his men had of heating the rails and wrapping them around trees to render them unusable gained the descriptive title of "Sherman's neckties." Throughout the war zone, whenever Union cavalry could tear up tracks and disrupt supplies to the Confederate army, it was done. Turning the tables, rebel partisan John S.

Mosby—also known as "The Gray Ghost"—was particularly adept at destroying rail lines and torching rolling stock with the letters "U. S." stenciled on the sides. The great battle at Gettysburg had its share of references to the railroad. There were three "railroad cuts" through ridges to the west of town which contained no ties or rails at the time, but still played an important part in the tactics of the first day's fighting. Most people know about the railroad cut over which the National Park Service tour route travels. In it were captured scores of Confederates during the see-sawing of lines on the first day's battle. And, of course, it was the railroad that brought President Lincoln to Gettysburg from Washington in November 1863 to deliver the Gettysburg Address, dedicating the National Cemetery, and re-dedicating the nation to the ongoing struggle for "a new birth of freedom."

Perhaps the saddest train ride of the war was the one that delivered the assassinated President Lincoln to Springfield, Illinois. He had come to Washington via the rails and was finally carried home to his grave via the train, having himself finally given "the last full measure of devotion."

And it is this train that provides us with one of the most bizarre ghost stories of the war: Upon certain spring nights, along a rural section of the track that runs from Chicago to Springfield, a hazy, indistinct form can be seen chugging slowly along the rails. A train...no, two trains...one leading the other. Those witnessing the sight find it strange: the engines and cars seem to have sprung from a different era, with broad cow-catchers and funnel smokestacks belching wood-smoke. The second train comes into view, and observers see by the last car that it is a funeral train. Peering through the windows of that car they can see the ancient coffin, strewn with flowers, and around it a military guard. But there is something strange and unearthly about the guards. Strange because they are dressed in military uniforms of a different era—the era of the Civil War. Unearthly, because inside the uniforms, standing at attention, are human skeletons. It is Lincoln's funeral train, passing once again along the route it passed so mournfully decades before. Its passing takes several minutes, but when the observers look at their watches, no time has gone by....

In the 1990s, Pioneer Lines, a large rail freight carrier headquartered in Peoria, Illinois, purchased a small, local railroad, the Gettysburg and Northern. What they didn't realize is that along with the rolling stock, locomotives, buildings, the rail right-of-way, and some abandoned cars, they also purchased… ghosts.

Workers on the railroad are usually no-nonsense kind of people. Most of them believe only what they can see, hear, or touch. That is why so many of them came away from a typical workday on the railroad with an uneasy feeling that there was more to the site than there should have been. It was because of what they had felt, heard, touched and seen that they realized the railroad—and especially the engine house—was haunted.

When you look at the history of the site upon which the railroad engine house and rails are located, it is easy to see why the place would harbor ghosts. Before there were any rails or ties, or an engine house, there was the battle. The Battle of Gettysburg began just a few hundred yards to the southwest of where the rails are laid and the engine house stands. As the battle drew the lumbering armies to Gettysburg, the natural terrain dictated the battle lines. Oak Ridge runs generally northward, an extension of Seminary Ridge, which, on the second and third day of the battle, became the main Confederate battle line. But on July 1, 1863, Oak Ridge was a Union position, at least until the Confederates overwhelmed the Union line and drove them, tumbling over Oak Ridge and across the fields to the east of it—right across the ground where the engine house now stands in the shadow of Oak Ridge.

And from the area of the engine house comes one of the most famous stories of the Battle of Gettysburg.

On the afternoon of July 1, 1863, the 16th Maine Infantry was fighting on the Oak Ridge line west of Gettysburg, a few hundred yards north of where the engine house was eventually constructed. Soon, the entire Union line north and west of Gettysburg imploded, with troops falling back through Gettysburg, heading for the high ground—Cemetery and Culp's Hills—south of the town. One regiment, however, was ordered to be the rear guard for the retreating Union Army. That regiment was the 16th Maine.

Every soldier, from the highest ranking officer to the lowliest private in the ranks knows what being the "rear guard" for a retreating army means. You will have only two courses of action: die where you stand or be captured and sent to prison pens like Andersonville, Georgia.

The commander of the 16th Maine was told to "Take the position and hold it at any cost." Colonel Tilden turned to the men of the 16th nearest him and said ominously, "You know what that means."

They fought like lions in their original position near the Mummasburg Road, but the huge Confederate scissors was closing on them inexorably. Outnumbered, overwhelmed, they began a slow retreat back down Oak Ridge. When they reached the easternmost railroad cut just a hundred yards from the current location of the engine house, they stopped. Surrounded, they heard the Confederates calling for them to give up and surrender their colors or be shot down.

As everyone who studies American History knows, their flags—the regimental colors—were the soul of the Civil War regiment: Their loss in battle was a shame the men were loath to bear; when a color-bearer was shot down men fought under fire for the honor of carrying the flag, only to be shot down themselves.

The enemy advanced and the men of the 16th Maine, instead of surrendering their flag, tore it to pieces and hid the fragments in their uniform blouses, then broke the staff. Of the 275 men of the 16th Maine who entered the fight, only 9 were killed and 52 wounded, but 162 were listed as missing or captured. Those were the ones sent to prisons in the south. Today, bits and pieces of that flag lie buried in the cemeteries at the former prison camps along with the bodies of the men of the 16th Maine who proved true to their colors unto—and even beyond—death.

Railroad Cut

No doubt some of the Union soldiers were shot down in the future footprint of the engine house. Some may have even been buried there, but no one knows for sure. The Confederate troops drove the Yankees through the town and the area became the rear of the Confederate lines and the dead there forgotten. Besides, Yankees were the enemy, and as long as the wind was blowing in the right direction, the rebels would leave their burial to their own comrades-in-arms. Some of the Union troops did return after the battle to find their wounded and bury their dead. For the most part, they were hasty burials indeed, with a piece of a cracker box for a headboard. After the rains came and the cows grazed, the flimsy boards were knocked down and the graves soon vanished. Yet they continue to emerge, the dead do, from the Pennsylvania clay around the engine house: The most recent soldier's remains found on the battlefield were discovered in 1996, between the easternmost and middle railroad cuts, just a few hundred yards from the engine house.

Looking at the engine house you wouldn't think it would be haunted. It's a relatively modern, all steel structure. But several investigations of the building and the surrounding area have proven that spirits, from the battle and from long-dead railroaders and passengers, may still inhabit the site.

My first trip to the engine house was to interview some of the railroaders. At first they proved to be a tough interview: No one wanted to be the first to admit he had experienced something from the Other World. But, after a while, they seemed to loosen up, especially after one of them said he had heard footsteps coming down the rickety wooden stairs inside the engine house when no one could be seen descending. One of the other fellows piped up: "You heard those, too? I thought I was the only one who heard them." It's always satisfying to get two independent sources to confirm a paranormal happening.

The men began to open up: Yes, others had heard the footsteps on the wooden stairs that led to an area over the office section of the engine house. As well, many times the men had been alerted by the alarm that someone had opened the back door and was coming toward the office area—but no one would appear. Then there was the un-nerving sound of someone walking on the "ballast" or stones that are spread on either side of the tracks. Someone would hear footsteps crunching along on the other side of the cars. They would investigate, only to find no one there. And workers cleaning the passenger cars would report hearing someone walking the length of the car. As the footsteps drew nearer, they would turn around to greet their fellow train worker, but no one else was in the car.

The stories I gathered that day during the interviews with somewhat reluctant witnesses convinced me that *something* was going on in the engine house that wasn't normal, and so a full paranormal investigation was scheduled.

The first team I accompanied spent several hours in the engine house filming and attempting to gather EVP. I actually recorded strange roars and garbled mumblings on my recorder when I attempted to address some members of the 16th Maine's color guard. I also got an enthusiastic roar when I requested the "rebel yell" from any Confederates present.

From that first investigation, I realized that there was enough activity in the engine house to warrant more investigations. We brought in a team composed of what I believe are the best paranormal investigators around today: Patty Wilson and Scott Crownover, of the Ghost Research Foundation; Investigative Medium Laine Crosby, who has been seen on the Travel Channel; Julie, another extremely gifted medium; and my wife Carol, who records much of the data and is an expert with the dowsing pendulum. During the investigation, Patty, who is also a sensitive, sensed a man on the back of one of the trains. He worked on the cars. She described him as a greasy, thin guy. "He likes to touch people," she related, "on the shoulder, their hair. He likes the women, but," and she quoted him as she heard him say, "not a lot of ladies come in here."

Interestingly enough, there was a woman who started talking to Patty concerning Patty going to the engine house about three days prior to the investigation. (When our mediums say that a man or woman has been "talking" to them, we always ask, "is this person dead or alive?" This one was dead.) Patty now feels that this was Tillie she encountered during the investigation.

The conversation between Patty and Tillie, according to our field notes, went something like this:

Tillie had worked at the railroad on and off for 20 years, from the late 1930s to the early 1950s. She had something to do with operations - she knew the trains. Jim, the manager of the railroad at the time, suggested that she might have been a clerk. Patty described her as a "tough old broad" and Tillie, according to Patty, thought that was funny. I asked if Tillie had been around on any of my previous visits to the engine house. Patty interpreted what she heard: "You came with a red-head before, but she couldn't see me." (I believe she was referring to Laine Crosby who is more of an empathic medium—one who "feels" things—rather than a clairvoyant—one who "sees" spirits.) "The blonde was good." (I believe she was referring this time to Julie, who is a blonde.)

Tillie has tried to talk to the men working here, but they can't hear her. Patty asked if she would be willing to try some EVP with me. She agreed.

During the EVP session, Patty could see Tillie leaning in towards the recorder to answer my questions. Afterwards she told Patty that she liked the EVP because she could still tell people what to do, like she did while working with the railroad, and they had to listen!

Sometime in 2005, I was approached by Frank May, an executive with Pioneer Lines Railroad. He had taken one of our Ghosts of Gettysburg Candlelight Walking Tours® and was impressed with the professionalism of our guides and fascinating stories. After numerous attempts, he finally got me to sit down with him and discuss the possibility of becoming partners in a new venture: The Ghost Train.

It was Halloween and I was signing books at the Depot of the Gettysburg and Northern Railroad. We were sending out two "Ghost Trains" that night and the first had just returned. Amy, one of our veteran guides, had returned to the depot and was listening as a wide-eyed young man came up to me. "Something happened to me on the train," he said. "I think it was a ghost." He said that, while he was riding in the aisle seat, he was touched on the shoulder. "It was like someone was walking down the aisle and needed to steady himself in the moving train. Someone leaned right on my shoulder, but I couldn't see him."

I was just about to go into my lecture about how suggestible we are when we're on a ghost tour, especially as teenagers, when the older man who was with him said, "Yes. I was right behind him and I felt it, too."

Multiple witnesses are what you look for to validate a story of the paranormal, and two had just dropped into my lap. The man was the boy's grandfather. He said that he saw the boy turn his head and look at his shoulder, then turn in his seat and say, "Grandpa, something just touched me on the shoulder." The grandfather was about to give the boy the same lecture I was, when he felt someone press down on his shoulder. "It felt like someone steadying himself against the rolling of the train, like a conductor, or passenger walking down the aisle."

Could it have been the "greasy, thin guy," Patty described, who "likes to touch people on the shoulder, the hair"?

During the off-season, Frank brought his friend Rob Conover, a gifted medium from Illinois who has been seen on several television programs, to investigate Gettysburg. Rob is a personable, talkative individual who shares his gifts freely. He did an investigation of our Ghosts of Gettysburg Headquarters building and confirmed what numerous investigations and psychics have said—it's haunted. He saw a little girl in the main lobby while I was video-taping the session. When we played it back, there is a distinct whistle during his conversation with the little girl, a whistle that came from no living person in the room.

Later, out at the engine house, we did an investigation with Rob who sensed that there were a number of soldiers trapped out there, who needed to cross over, to go to the light. After assisting several to do just that, he felt there was one who was reluctant to leave this earthly plane. He was what Rob called, a "preacher." Not necessarily an ordained minister, but one who felt the call to spread the gospel to his fellow soldiers before he was killed in the battle. His concern for the souls of the men he cared for was so strong it apparently held him to the area around the engine house for some 14 decades before Rob finally contacted him. I was recording on my digital recorder Rob's attempts to talk the preacher over to the other side. Rob tells him that he can go on over now, that the men he helped are over there too. On the recording you hear Rob say, "Go on, Preacher. You're almost there. You might as well go the rest of the way around." When I reviewed the tape later that night, after his exhortations to the preacher, the same word came twice from the small digital recorder as an EVP. It was as if the preacher was finally seeing what he'd spent so much time telling his fellow soldiers about. "Heaven," a disembodied voice calls out from the recorder. And later, again, "Heaven!"

Rob's son, Julie, Laine and I were relaxing after the investigation. It was after dark and Julie suddenly pointed to some bushes lining the track behind some parked freight cars. "Look," she said. "Can you see all the people?" Laine peered into the darkness. "Yes," she said. "What are they all doing over there, this late at night? They must be students." (Gettysburg College lies just beyond the tracks.) "Why are they all out here?"

Julie said, "No. They're not students. Look more closely." "They must be students," Laine said. "But what are they all doing there." "Look more closely," Julie said. "See. They have no legs." "Oh, my God," Laine said as she realized they were not modern students she was seeing, but literally dozens of partially materialized ghosts.

Although the railroaders continue to be no-nonsense skeptics, other strange events have plagued workers in the Engine House.

One worker, who had never had a paranormal experience in his life, had several in the engine house that he will never forget. He had just come on the job and was unaware of all the stories of the place. The lights were on, but he saw, between the parked engines a misty, translucent form begin to take shape. At first he thought it was fog or mist, confused as to why it would be inside a structure. Then, as he watched, the amorphous form moved, as if it had a mind of its own.

Another time he was in the engine house alone and saw another amorphous mass form before his eyes. It began to move towards him. He moved towards it, actually wanting to touch it to see if it was damp, like mist, but it moved away from him. He backed off and it moved back towards him as if it was curious. He moved towards it again and again it moved away, finally moving down the track, disappearing through the engine house wall. He began carrying a camera with him and captured some remarkable shots of paranormal energies forming and dissipating.

Engine House Interior Photo Courtesy of Jim Jacobs

The same worker had been on a few of our investigations and had heard the story of Tillie, how she had worked on the railroad for a number of years. One night, he was getting ready to leave and noticed his coffee cup on his desk.

Normally, he'll clean up his desk for the next morning, but this night he was especially tired and figured he'd take care of the cup in the morning. When he arrived the next morning and got to his desk, he realized that the cup, which had been in the middle of his desk, had been moved to the side. Since he was one of the first in the building that morning, he was perplexed. He asked the other worker who had come in with him if he had used his desk and moved the cup. The other worker's confused expression told him he hadn't.

That night, he purposefully placed his coffee cup in the middle of his desk, just to see what would happen. The next morning, he got in to work especially early, before anyone else. The cup had been moved to the side. He decided to experiment. He placed the cup in the middle of the desk and wrote a note. The note said, "Move it to the other side." He was purposefully unspecific as to what the object was and to which side of the desk the object was to be moved, just in case a fellow worker was absent-mindedly moving the cup. He even placed the note face-down on the desk. When he arrived at work the next morning, the cup had been moved...to the other side of the desk where it had never been before.

During one of the Mysterious Journeys weekends when we bring groups of people through the engine house, we decided to try and contact someone else Patty Wilson felt was with us. Actually, we almost had no choice. Patty said that someone kept bothering her to talk with us. Not surprisingly, she unspecifically said it was a "trainman." I had been busy asking questions of other entities, and changing our groups around, when, all of a sudden, there was a collective gasp from the group. A traffic barrel that had been standing at the back end of the engine house had been forcibly knocked over, as if someone had kicked it. The only problem was no one was near it when it happened. The manager of the railroad, and a couple of others, walked over to the barrel to inspect it, and could find no reason for it to fall on its side. It had been sitting in its original position for a week or so.

More stories continue to come from the railroaders. One was working on an engine when his eye caught some movement across the tracks. As his eyes focused, he saw a Styrofoam cup levitate from inside of a wooden box, float above it for several seconds, then drop back into the box, as if some phantom railroader had needed a quick sip of coffee before he went on duty. The worker rushed over to the bench to see if he could detect any breeze that might have lifted the cup in such an odd manner, but the doors to the engine house were all closed and there was no breeze.

In 2010 during one of the Mysterious Journeys Weekends, our group was split into three investigations. One was in the diner car that was parked outside of the engine house. Scott Crownover and Sam Biestline, one of the workers on the railroad, were with the group in the diner car, as was my wife Carol. Suddenly, they heard an unearthly boom that seemed to come from just outside the car.

It was so intense that it shook the heavy car. Sam and Scott inspected outside of the car to see if a large amount of snow had dislodged from somewhere and landed on the roof—but there was no snow on or around the car. A month later, Sam, Scott and Carol were leading another group of investigators through the car when another ear-splitting boom rocked the car. Subsequent examination of the exterior revealed nothing that would have caused it.[1]

Orbs on Ceiling of Dining Car During Dowsing Session

There is no doubt that during every one of the Mysterious Journeys Weekends something paranormal occurs. I had finished giving the history of the engine house and led the group inside, past a huge, black engine on the track nearest the door. Laine had already been in the building for a while and had climbed onto the engine because she had felt an energy there. When she came down she told her impressions: that the locomotive had been used at one time to pull a car filled with corpses, the victims of a flood. (Not the famous Johnstown Flood, but another natural disaster.) She felt that some of them were still there since they had not been given a proper burial. As we all stood there, I began to hear the impossible.

From the engine, noises began to emanate. I listened and realized the noises were similar to the sounds when Laine was walking along the catwalk on the engine—footsteps on metal, like the sound of someone walking on a metal fire escape. I was convinced that someone from our group was walking on the engine. I began to walk over to the front of the massive locomotive to suggest that they get down since it can be very dangerous that high off the ground.

(The whole place is dangerous; participants all must sign a waiver before they are allowed to investigate it.) As I rounded the engine, expecting to see one of our investigators, I saw...nothing. No one was on the engine. I turned to some of our group and asked them if they could hear the sounds as well. Every one of them answered in the affirmative. Knowing that the huge, steel engines sometimes make noise as they cool down in the shade of the engine house, I approached the manager of the railroad. I asked him how long that particular engine had been in the engine house.

"About a month," was his answer.

"Is there anything in that engine that would cause it to make a sound like someone walking on it?"

"No," he replied. "We've drained all the fluids out of it. It's just a big hunk of metal sitting there."

I returned to the Engine House, no wiser as to the source of the sounds than when I left. The walking sounds emanating from the locomotive began to slowly diminish until, as Patty and Laine crossed the last soul over to the light, they ceased completely.

Is it the incredible steel matrix of rails, like some gargantuan antenna, that draws the spirit energies to the engine house? Or is it merely the souls of soldiers, shattered in battle, losing their lives, their futures, their families and for some, their very identities that keeps or draws them to the east side of Oak Ridge in Gettysburg to roam amongst the vehicles that, in their times, were the ultimate in luxurious travel?

83

THE PHANTOM BATTALION

*...all human experience is valid, or real to the percipient. Only the
interpretation or meaning given to the experience is subject to question.*
 –Dr. Edgar Mitchell, Astronaut, *The Way of the Explorer*

Little Round Top is perhaps the place on the Gettysburg Battlefield where
Civil War tactics are the most obvious, and most illustrative of why armies
strive to capture the high ground.

Although the height to the south—Big Round Top—is higher, it was
wooded at the time of the battle, so artillery could not be brought to the top.
Historians have argued that, if a regiment of good southern backwoodsmen
could have been marched to the summit with axes, they could have cleared
it for the big guns. The point is moot. Little Round Top *had* been cleared the
autumn before the battle by the Weikert family for firewood. Their heating needs
provided the Union Army with a cleared field of fire with which to dominate
the southern end of the field.

Historians also argue that if Confederates could have taken Little Round
Top, *they* could have dominated the battlefield with *their* artillery, and Gettysburg
would have been a Confederate victory, perhaps leading to the end of the war
and Southern independence. Other historians deny that Confederate artillery
could have been brought that far from where it was on Seminary Ridge, or that
it could have stayed on Little Round Top long enough to destroy the Union line.

Historians do agree that they came close. During the early afternoon of
July 2, 1863, Major General Daniel Sickles, unhappy with his position in the
low ground on Cemetery Ridge, pushed his entire Third Corps toward the
Emmitsburg Road, without orders, to the higher ground near the Peach Orchard.
Union commander George Meade personally rode out to find out what Sickles
was doing. In a heated discussion—Meade was nicknamed "Old Snapping
Turtle" for his temperament—Meade chastised Sickles for advancing his troops
without orders. Sickles asked if Meade wanted him to return his troops to their
original position. At that moment a Confederate shell burst over their heads,
nearly killing Sickles and the commander of the entire Federal army. "Don't
bother," Meade shot back, "the enemy will save you the trouble."

Sickles exposed line endured a half hour cannonade. Then came the
onslaught. Confederate General James Longstreet's troops advanced and

84

drove the Yankees from the Peach Orchard, through the Wheatfield and out of Devil's Den. Here is where Sickles' mistake loomed: where Sickles' line ended at Devil's Den, Longstreet's line extended beyond it. Some Confederates actually climbed the back side of Big Round Top, placing them in a position to advance and take Little Round Top, which was, at the time, unoccupied by any Federal troops, other than a few signalmen and an engineering officer. But the Confederates had advanced before their canteens had been filled; the day was hot and the southern slope of Big Round Top is, in some places, a hand-over-hand climb. The Southerners got to the summit and collapsed from exhaustion to a man. A young staff officer rode up and implored them to continue their advance. He was roundly cursed.

In the meantime, on Little Round Top, the engineering officer, Major General G. K. Warren, was watching the battle play out to the west. He also noticed the fighting in Devil's Den was not going their way. Some sources say that he became suspicious of the wooded slope of Big Round Top and ordered a Federal cannon to fire a shot into the woods. As the shell crashed into the treetops, Confederate infantry inadvertently ducked and the filtered sunlight reflected off their bayonets and musket barrels in a long, glittering line all the way up to the top of Big Round Top. He looked around and realized he and the few signalmen were the only friendly troops on Little Round Top. He also suddenly realized the importance of the hill should the Confederates take it.

Warren rushed down the slope of Little Round Top and ordered the first Union troops he found to the summit. They were just in time. They ran headlong into the Confederates from Big Round Top who had caught their breath and were on their way to capturing the key to the Union position. Fighting raged up and down the slopes of Little Round Top and in the valley between the two hills. Finally, Confederates were driven from Little Round Top and it was secured by the Union forces.

Within a day or two all the soldiers were gone from Gettysburg, marching towards new battlefield horrors as they left behind the horrors of this one. But it seems as though one battalion didn't leave Gettysburg—a battalion of the dead.

The original ghost story comes from one of the older park rangers at Gettysburg. Its genesis is in the late 1950s, before reenacting the Civil War era became such a passionate pastime for so many. It's the original date that gives the story its authentic ring.

There was a group of dignitaries touring the battlefield with a park ranger. They had been to the sites of the opening shots and General Reynolds's death, past the field of Pickett's Charge, and to the summit of the most prominent feature on the Gettysburg Battlefield, Little Round Top. The ranger recounted the story of the fighting on the eminence and they were about to leave the summit when one of the dignitaries pointed out something coming out of the woods.

Before them, in full military regalia, was a battalion-sized Civil War unit. The men marched out of the woods on Hauck's Ridge, wheeled, halted, advanced, and performed a few other maneuvers, then marched back into the woods. The dignitaries were so impressed that the National Park Service would put on such a performance just for their benefit, they thanked their escort vociferously. Now, they wished to thank the chief ranger in person. The ranger must drive them to the headquarters so they might do that.

Once in the chief ranger's office, they shook his hand, and remarked over and over again, how wonderful such a surprise demonstration was to someone as important as they were. Thanking him over and over, they finally left the chief ranger's office. Both rangers looked at each other and shrugged. No group had been arranged for, and no armed and uniformed groups were even on the park that day. The wonderful demonstration for the important officials had been arranged by a power quite beyond that of the National Park Service.

Now, if that were the only sighting of this large group of soldiers, appearing in the area below Little Round Top, marching with practiced military precision, then virtually vanishing somewhere in the woods, one could relegate it to an aberration of the mind—or in the case of the dignitaries, aberrations of the minds. But the strange vision has been seen several times since, of the group of soldiers visiting from somewhere beyond the battlefield, that has come to be known as the "Phantom Regiment" or "Phantom Battalion."

A man and his friend were visiting the battlefield in June 1975. He, unfortunately, had broken his leg, and the trip to Gettysburg was a pause in the boredom of being laid up with a full leg cast. The National Park Service Visitor Center was jammed with schoolchildren on the obligatory senior trip to Gettysburg, so they decided to drive around the battlefield. They were approaching the Wheatfield, the "maelstrom of death," so named by the soldiers themselves. At the far end of the Wheatfield, they saw what they believed to be a large reenactment group of about "100 to 150" Union soldiers, marching in formation, wheeling left and right, moving away from them until they were out of sight. They were impressed and decided to check at the Visitor Center to see when the next demonstration was scheduled. They inquired about the unit and were told by a ranger that no reenactment groups were on the battlefield that day. The ranger also said, with remarkable candor, that what they might have seen was the "Phantom Battalion," a ghostly unit, occasionally seen in that area.

The two men didn't quite believe the ranger when his explanation encompassed the paranormal, so they decided to investigate themselves. They returned to the Wheatfield to try and spot so large a group of reenactors. Certainly, they must be camped nearby, or at least came in busses that would have to be parked somewhere. Certainly there would be individuals, or smaller groups moving around the area since the "demonstration" was over.

Within an hour of having seen the first "demonstration," they parked near the Wheatfield, but saw nothing. No vehicles, no stragglers, nothing. Curiosity got the better of them and the one man decided to check out the field. Surely, with that large a number of men marching, there must be some sign they had been there.

The Wheatfield

The man with the broken leg waited in the car. Finally, his friend came back, looking "a little pale and green around the gills." He reported that he found no footprints, no broken blades of grass or wheat, not a sign that seven-score men had tramped over a fresh field. "It was like they hadn't even been there!"

A number of things in the story lead to its veracity. First, the large number of soldiers involved. Even today, after the hobby of reenacting has reached its highest popularity in years, it would be difficult to arrange for 150 reenactors to show up on the Gettysburg Battlefield for a brief march-around. Many of the "units" can muster barely 20 to 30 participants, even for the massive Memorial Day or Remembrance Day Parades in Gettysburg. One hundred and fifty reenactors driving into position onto the battlefield would require three to four buses or a minimum of 30 cars. The ever alert rangers of the National Park at Gettysburg would certainly have noticed 150 armed and uniformed men entering or leaving the park…as long it was by normal—and not paranormal—means.

Other reports of the "Phantom Battalion" have entered into the ghost lore of Gettysburg, all reporting about the same thing. The following is typical.

A woman, her son, and their dog were on a dawn excursion onto the battlefield. They had just turned off of the Emmitsburg Road onto the Wheatfield Road and were cresting the hill at the Peach Orchard when they saw a large unit of Union soldiers marching across the misty field. She stopped the car to watch, but something seemed out of place. Their dog was growling, apparently seeing the same thing the humans were. Impressed with what they thought was a crack reenactment unit in an early-morning drill, they watched for several minutes. The group of soldiers, in perfect alignment, wheeled, about-faced, marched around, and then did something no reenactment unit has yet to accomplish. As some joggers crested the hill, the soldiers vanished into thin air.

The dog growling at the "Phantom Battalion" is more important than it would first seem. When humans witness a paranormal event, we do it with numerous explanations as to why what we are seeing cannot be real: *something under my contacts; my imagination; I must be hallucinating; too much to drink.* Animals, especially dogs, simply "alert". If they alert to something, it must be there; they must be seeing something. That is why accounts of animals "seeing" ghosts—and they are numerous—are indicative of the existence of ghosts.

Could it be that man's best friend is also his best "ghost detector?"

MORE MYSTERIES ON OAK RIDGE

One's thoughts, especially when amplified by intent or emotion, leave an imprint on matter, that is, will directs all energy. Previous thought forms may remain as fields in places such as buildings, powerfully affecting susceptible people who resonate with them.

–Valerie Hunt, *Infinite Mind*

When World War II was over, the young men who fought, as if rejoicing to have made it through the most costly war in history, married, bought houses and cars, started a "baby-boom," and began to do what only the rich had done before the war: take vacations. One of the places they went—young warriors visiting where older warriors fought and fell—was Gettysburg.

Early on, people in Gettysburg merely rented out a room in their homes to the visiting strangers. Later, "Tourist Homes" appeared around town. Some locals on the outskirts of town opened campgrounds. A few far-sighted entrepreneurs built "Motor-courts" in the early 1950s when visitors wanted something nicer. To these they later added swimming pools and changed their names to "motels." As tourism to Gettysburg became an industry, larger hotels began to spring up. Then, in the 1990s, Gettysburg went "back to the future."

The Bed & Breakfast seemed a throwback to the "Tourist Home" days, except with modern conveniences. And Gettysburg proved an ideal setting for "B & Bs."

Bed & Breakfasts that are in town are within walking distance of most attractions; those out of town are usually situated near battle sites. But whether they are in town or out, they share one thing with many of the other buildings in Gettysburg: They were either involved in the battle as hospitals or sit on land that may have absorbed the blood of American soldiers. Therefore, they share one other trait: They may very well be haunted.

One Bed & Breakfast ideally located for both the casual visitor and the avid ghost hunter has been rather quiet about its ghosts. I have written about The Doubleday Inn before as the scene of a number of mysterious, unexplainable happenings.[1] It sits on Oak Ridge with just a handful of other private houses. It sits, in fact, across the road from one of the most historically haunted sites in all of Gettysburg: Iverson's Pits.

On the sultry afternoon of July 1, the Confederate brigade of Brigadier General Alfred Iverson, North Carolina regiments one and all, advanced in battle line from their position across the Mummasburg Road. Two other brigades, supposed to protect his flanks, had been repulsed earlier. In spite of the lack of protection, Iverson ordered his 1,400 men forward without skirmishers with the un-military entreaty, "Give them hell, boys!" Their march was eerily un-vexed until they reached a point less than eighty yards from a stone wall along Oak Ridge. Suddenly, Union soldiers rose from behind the wall and poured a volley down their flank, which killed and wounded hundreds in the blink of an eye.

Lieutenant George W. Grant of the 88th Pennsylvania told of the one-sided affair in a speech nearly 35 years later: "Behind our stronghold we quietly awaited the enemy to come within short range, a word of caution being passed along the line 'to await command and aim low.' When the enemy had reached within about fifty yards of our front a death-dealing flame belched forth, staggering them momentarily, but they soon sought safety in flight, leaving the ground strewn with the dead and wounded."[2]

Scores fell in that first volley. A Confederate soldier was detailed to break down fences for the movement of artillery on Oak Ridge when he came across the grisly aftermath of the first few seconds of firing: "There were [with]in a few feet of us, by actual count, seventy-nine (79) North Carolinians lying dead in a straight line. I stood on their right and looked down their line. It was perfectly dressed. Three had fallen to the front, the rest had fallen backward; yet the feet of all these dead men were in a perfectly straight line."[3]

According to Lt. Grant, the survivors of the first fusillade retreated some 150 yards to a shallow, dry creek bed, but it gave them little shelter and no means of escape. The Tarheels attempted an assault on the Union line but were compelled to resume their spot of dubious safety. The Union troops were relentless, calmly loading and firing from behind the stone wall until the survivors waved handkerchiefs on ramrods.

General Iverson thought, mistakenly, that his whole brigade was filled with cowards, lying down and surrendering. The reality was some 500 were casualties and the rest quickly becoming casualties.

The Union troops behind the wall rushed the North Carolinians and captured a large number of Iverson's Brigade and a number of regimental colors. They didn't spend too much time in the open field; Confederates were regrouping and the farm fields of John Forney could be just as deadly for Yankees as they had been for Rebels.

Again, Lt. Grant recalled three and a half decades later with crystal clarity, his brigade began to run low on ammunition, resorting to robbing the cartridge boxes of the dead and wounded. While the stone wall provided some protection, "a head or body shown above the wall became a target, and many fell dead or wounded."

Yet with that danger, Colonel Charles Wheelock of the 97th New York stood defiantly waving a captured Confederate flag, taunting the enemy. Even after he was ordered to stop by Brigadier General Baxter he refused. Finally, he was placed under arrest. He called to a captain in his ranks to hold the rebel flag and ran his sword through it tearing it from the staff as a final insult to the Confederates. He and the captain stood waving the tattered flag and staff until a Confederate, having had enough, put a bullet into the forehead of the captain killing him.[4]

The horror was to go on. Union supports came up commanded by Brigadier General Gabriel Paul. Paul followed his brigade upon horseback until they were in position along Oak Ridge near the Mummasburg Road. A minie ball, whistling in at about 900 feet per second, struck Paul in the right temple, destroying his right eye and optic nerve and continued on to exit through his left eye socket, destroying that eyeball. From that moment on Paul was sightless. The wound later affected his sense of smell and hearing.

When the Union Army retreated, he was left on the field for dead and he was originally reported in the Cincinnati newspaper as having been killed at Gettysburg, but for twenty years after the war he was seen very much alive, walking holding the arm of his second wife almost daily until the wound he took at Gettysburg eventually killed him. He had suffered violent pains in his head and epileptic convulsions until May 1886, when he lapsed into a coma and died. He had two daughters and, surprisingly for a Union officer, had owned two slaves before the war.[5]

Vicinity of Iverson's Pits

Iverson's men, buried where they were slain, remained in their unconsecrated graves until the 1870s, when what was left of them was removed and taken South, leaving depressions in the ground known to this day as "Iverson's Pits." While their grisly remains were returned home and the "Pits" have succumbed to the leveling of erosion and the farmer's plow, it seems that some part of them has stayed over the long century-and-a-half since their last conscious thought was of panic and mortal fear. The legend is that Farmer Forney could not get his Pennsylvania Dutch farmhands to work in the area as dusk neared: they repeated fantastic stories of hearing bugles and orders shouted, of the thudding of soft lead bullets into flesh over and over, and of the death-screams of men fighting the very last enemy they would ever face on this earth: the Grim Reaper himself.

As Forney's workers tried to avoid the area, modern paranormal researchers are drawn to it and have recorded photographs and EVP at the site of Iverson's Pits. The results are spine-chilling in at least one example. After the researcher gives a blessing, "God be with you," from the modern recorder comes the remnant of one man's final death agony: a blood-curdling scream.

Iverson's men would be avenged, however. Later that afternoon, Confederates would push the Union troops in ignominious retreat, off Oak Ridge, running through the fields northwest of Gettysburg, beyond the town and, inadvertently, onto one of the finest defensive positions in modern warfare.

Doubleday Inn Photo Courtesy of Darlene Perrone

In 2006, Christine and Todd Thomas purchased the Doubleday Inn, a Bed & Breakfast located upon Oak Ridge. Though the Doubleday Inn was built many years after the battle that left the area around and under it strewn with corpses, it seems the building may have absorbed some of the energy from the slain as they were shuffling off their mortal coils.

The lovely spacious house was built specifically for the Reverend Abraham (Lutheran Theological Seminary at Gettysburg, Class of 1898) and Agnes Longanecker by their children in 1939. It was part of the Forney Farm during the battle. The Rev. Longanecker died in 1957. The house was used as apartments for a while supplying housing for Park Rangers or students. The Longanecker sisters lived there as well.

When Christine and Todd bought the Doubleday Inn, it had already been a B & B for a number of years. It was named after Major General Abner Doubleday who took over command of the Union Army's First Corps after the death of Major General John F. Reynolds. Most of old staff stayed. The Thomas's discovered that the housekeepers have certain rooms they don't like to go in. An older housekeeper who hasn't worked there in a while, came back and told the story of what paranormal investigators classify as a warp, or tear in the fabric of time.

During the last year the former owners were there, a group rented the entire house. The group didn't tell them until the last minute that they were a paranormal investigation group. The innkeeper's wife was not "into" the ghost scene and got upset when she found out. She left town for a weekend in Washington D.C., and left her husband in charge.

The group began its investigation in the field behind the Inn which is now orchard planted by the National Park Service. They took pictures outside and recorded lots of those mysterious orbs. They asked the owner what he thought of pictures, but the innkeeper kept deferring. He was not really a believer in ghosts, so he kept changing the subject to the incredible history of the area around the Inn.

The next night the whole group went out to Iverson's Pits to investigate. While they were gone, the innkeeper went out to the woodpile…and apparently entered into another world.

He had just picked up a piece of wood when he heard a loud bang, then more loud cracks, like gunfire. He looked up and it was as if some unseen hand had parted the veil of Time. Suddenly, he was watching the battle taking place, recreating itself before his eyes. Men in Union blue were running past him. It was the panicked Union retreat all over again! Suddenly a figure loomed in front of him and a soldier ran right into him. But instead of knocking him down, he passed right through him.

Although it was a warm night, he got a sudden, inexplicable chill and went inside. He called his wife, but got no sympathy from her.

The next day his wife returned from Washington and went to her bedroom in the owner's quarters. There she found a button—a Union soldier's uniform button—on her side of the bed. Within the year, the Inn was for sale.

Christine, the current co-owner, has had a few experiences since they purchased the Inn. She often gets the feeling someone is watching her. She will sometimes see things out of the corner of her eye, which is fairly common for a paranormal sighting.[6]

Shortly after Todd and Christine took over the Inn on June 21, 2006, Christine and the Inn dog Molly went upstairs to the Gabriel Paul Room on the third floor, named after the tragic Union officer blinded within sight of where the Doubleday Inn now stands. The air conditioning had been on and the room was comfortably cool. Christine knew the maids had been in earlier and had made up the bed. However, she noticed an impression on the bed as if someone had sat down on it after it had been made. Suddenly the dog stopped, looked at the spot and started growling. Both hurried back downstairs.

Later, the guests who were to stay in the Gabriel Paul Room arrived. As Christine escorted the guests upstairs and opened the door she realized that the room was stiflingly hot. She noticed that both windows in the room were open the same amount. The curtains, which are normally held tightly on the rods, were pushed open. The illogical part about it was that no one had been up there to open the windows or move the curtains since she and the dog had checked the room...except, perhaps, whoever sat to rest upon the bed.

But over the years Christine and Todd have realized something: Nearly every bed in the Inn has had depressions that needed to be smoothed after they've already been made up. The Paul Room seems to be where most stories emanate. Guests staying there ask, "Who were the little girls playing upstairs?" Occupants of the room named after the blinded general will hear children playing marbles overhead. There are no little girls upstairs. It is a physical impossibility, since the Paul Room is the renovated attic of the Inn.

Though General Paul died in 1886 in Washington D.C., he (and his family) apparently has an affinity for the room named after him. In the fall of 2007, a young girl who was staying at the Inn saw a little girl whom she said "lived in the attic." The young girl continued to talk about her, to the delight of her parents who marveled at the wonderful imagination of their daughter. The little girl in the attic was named "Bea" and their daughter said she spent time playing with her.

All this could be written off as the delightful story from a little girl with an overactive imagination if it wasn't for a visit to Gettysburg by Tom Paul, a descendent of General Paul, who stayed in the Paul Room. Tom documented the fact that with his second wife (whom he had married in 1858) General Paul had two little girls; one was named Beatrice. Could this be the little girl named "Bea" that has been heard playing in the "attic"? Could this be the child-like apparition that is so realistic that a young girl can play with her?

Other happenings not-of-this-world continue in and around the Doubleday Inn. Guests will hear horses clopping by in front of the Inn. Visitors smell cigar smoke on the side porch when no one can be seen smoking. People hear cannons being fired close by the house. All of which happened in the vicinity of where the Inn stands today...but fifteen decades before it even existed.

There are at least two documented accounts of a Civil War "courier"— who people think must be a reenactor—riding "hell bent for leather" down Oak Ridge, and stopping at the Inn. When the people get to the Inn, within seconds of seeing the rider, he is gone—no horse, no rider.

The woods just across the street from the Doubleday Inn are known by historians as Sheads' Woods; to paranormalists, they are the "Haunted Woods." It is in those woods where two sisters and their mother had the most frightening experience of their lives. Late one winter evening they heard strange noises coming from the woods. They thought it was an odd time to have a party, and upon inspection, began to hear sounds that definitely did not come from a party. As they walked deeper into the woods, they realized from the agonized screams and moans, they were about to come upon a Civil War Hospital. They left the woods before reaching the spot from where the horrifying sounds came.

The owners continue to experience strange, unexplainable happenings. In January 2008, Christine was in their office and Todd in the basement. Todd was surprised to hear a music box playing a classic melody of a lullaby. The box played through the song twice. The mystery, perhaps to be solved only by an explanation that encompasses Another World, is that there is no music box in the Doubleday Inn and nothing else in the house that could produce the sweet children's song Todd heard.[7]

GENERAL LEE'S HEADQUARTERS

Thought and mind have been said to precede the existence of matter, to continue through matter, and to exist at the termination of matter albeit in new forms. This implies that thought and mind do not disintegrate because they are not subject to physical laws.

–Valerie Hunt, *Infinite Mind*

If you were Robert E. Lee on the afternoon of July 1, 1863 riding over Herr's Ridge with your staff officers, your military mind would be on overdrive.

Historians have a general idea of his plans for the summer campaign of 1863. According to Lee's trusted subordinate General James Longstreet, Lee wanted a campaign that was strategically offensive, but tactically defensive. We know at least two things from his contemporary correspondence to his officers, written mostly by Charles Marshall, Lee's military secretary, during the march northward throughout June: first, that the continuance of his campaign into the enemy's country would depend upon his troops gathering supplies as much as anything else; second, he did not want to bring on a large battle as his divisions were spread across much of south-central Pennsylvania. One could get the idea that Lee saw this summer campaign as a gigantic raid into enemy territory for supplies—cattle, horses, fodder, and foodstuffs for his army to transport into the south.

But what he saw once he got to the ridges west of the town of Gettysburg that afternoon must have changed his mind completely.

Historians have often pondered why Lee altered his campaign plan from not wanting to fight a pitched battle to fighting one of the most tactically offensive battles in his military life. It may have to do with what he saw when he was overlooking the small crossroads town for the first time.

Picture it: You are the commander of the entire Confederate Army of Northern Virginia, rolling off several magnificent victories and attempting, for a summer campaign, to take the war out of Virginia and the Shenandoah Valley so that the farmers there can get the first good crop growing in the ground since the war started. You're apprehensive because, since you left the little village of Cashtown to the west, you've been hearing the sound of the guns—musketry, but more worrisome, artillery, meaning your troops have run into more than just local militia. Large numbers of prisoners and your own wounded passing by you on their way to the rear tell you that indeed there is a big fight going on just ahead, and you have no idea how it's going because, the last time you checked, your army was spread out, thirty miles to the Susquehanna River near Harrisburg, another thirty miles to that same river to the east. You issued orders to concentrate on the little town you are riding toward—what was the name again?—Gettysburg. But you cannot be sure they will arrive in time at the battle that seems to be raging to secure victory or stave off defeat. Then you crest a ridge nearing the town and you see an amazing thing: your army is driving the enemy from the ridge before them. Your staff says the buildings on it belong to a Lutheran Seminary and you continue your pace until you reach it. Suddenly, you witness your army's two wings are coming together like a giant shears, driving the panicked Union Army before it, from the high ground, through the town.

The Union line is crumbling before your very eyes with Yankees running across yards and through the streets. Small pockets of troops attempt to stop your soldiers but soon dissolve. It's very similar to the battle you just fought at Chancellorsville two months before, except without General Jackson. Now, being so far north, so close to Harrisburg and Philadelphia, capturing one or both of those major cities just might bring an end to this wicked war and secure independence for the South. Suddenly, you change your battle plans from wanting to avoid a general engagement this far north to striking the enemy a death blow.

You look to your right, to the south, and see past the Seminary buildings a long ridge, possibly a good position to hold for an upcoming battle. To the left, across the road is a small stone house. Beyond that, past a railroad cut, is another ridge from which the Yankees are retreating. You call to your aide, Colonel Walter Taylor and send a message to General Ewell to press "those people" and gain the heights beyond the town. Perhaps you ponder: if this becomes the battle that ends this war, this may be, one day, an important place, the site of the battle that won the War for Southern Independence. Who can tell…?

Of course, Gettysburg did become a place of great importance, but not in the way Robert E. Lee would have wanted. Instead, it became the site of the victory that ended the dream of Confederate Independence.

Lee could never have imagined that Gettysburg would someday be a National Military Park, thanks mostly to the Union veterans themselves encouraging local organizations and governmental departments alike to purchase and preserve lands upon which they fought and upon which their comrades bled and died.

Nor could he have envisioned the popularity that park would eventually have with the American public.

Estimates of up to 1.6 million people visit Gettysburg every year. Those people need places to eat and sleep and things to do to educate themselves on the import of the great battle that once consumed the lives of their ancestors, so Gettysburg has grown to accommodate them. Museums have come and gone over the years; rooms in private homes were first to accommodate visitors; campgrounds and later hotels sprang up, then, responding to individual ownership of the automobile, motor courts, which would later be called motels. One of the most enduring motels is literally on the first day's battlefield. I have written about it in other *Ghosts of Gettysburg* books, documenting the sounds, in the middle of the night, of cannons booming and of items being moved by unseen hands. The Quality Inn at General Lee's Headquarters on Buford Avenue has a long history of providing visitors and tourists with a wonderful experience. It is truly "on the battlefield," with cannons marking the position of Stewart's Union Battery of Artillery literally in their back yard.

From the site, one can overlook almost the entire first day's battlefield, from McPherson's Ridge where the major fighting started between Buford's Union cavalry and Harry Heth's Confederate infantry to Oak Ridge across the rail road cut, down into the town of Gettysburg. The famous photo of three Confederate prisoners standing by a log breastwork was taken directly across the street. Perhaps most importantly, Confederate commander Robert E. Lee had his headquarters on this part of Seminary Ridge.

Timothy Smith, a Licensed Battlefield Guide, produced an excellent book called, *The Story of Lee's Headquarters: Gettysburg, Pennsylvania*. He details the fighting near the Lutheran Theological Seminary and the Widow Thompson House, now known as Lee's Headquarters, around which the modern motel has grown. In the text he reproduces a segment of what is known as the Elliot Map, showing purported burials in the area of the Thompson House and in the area where the modern motel now stands. Both Union and Confederate (but mostly Confederate) burials appear to have occurred, if not in the vicinity of the motel, then underneath where the motel now stands.[1]

First, some history, then a little paranormal theory.

Virtually every soldier killed in the Battle of Gettysburg was buried at least twice. First the bodies were gathered together and interred on the battlefield near where they fell, usually in very shallow graves, sometimes marked with crude, wooden headboards if identity could be established. After several weeks, being buried in their blankets for coffins without embalming, the bodies swelled from gases and began to decompose. For the housewives of Gettysburg the graves became a nightmare scenario: arms popped out of the earth of their kitchen gardens, the grisly, leathered hands seemingly beckoning to join the soldier in his sepulcher; human heads, the flesh slowly sloughing from the skull with larvae and insects crawling throughout leered at them, apparently mocking the civilians' lives the soldiers gave theirs to protect. The women could stand it no more.

Their husbands petitioned Governor Curtain in Harrisburg who appointed a local attorney, David Wills, to procure land for the consolidated re-burial of the scattered soldiers' remains. Wills purchased 17 acres of orchard and cornfield on Cemetery Hill and exhumations began. Burials paused on November 19, 1863, for the dedication and consecration of the new National Cemetery by President Abraham Lincoln. Burials continued until the ground was too hard to dig, then resumed again in the spring. Finally, the soldiers lay in consecrated entombment.

At least, the *Union* soldiers did.

Confederates, in 1863, were the enemy and no enemy soldiers were to be buried in the National Cemetery next to the loyal soldiers they may have killed. So the Confederates remained buried on the battlefield in their hasty graves until 1870-71 when exhumations began, allegedly to be paid for by Southern ladies' societies.

One of the criteria recognized by paranormalists for a haunting is an unconsecrated burial. Union soldiers were buried in unconsecrated graves until their re-burial in the consecrated National Cemetery. Confederates remained on the battlefield in unconsecrated graves for another six or seven years. As well, it is known that not all the bodies were recovered; some may still rest— uneasily—in unknown, unconsecrated makeshift mausoleums. The most recent remains were found in 1996 within sight of the Quality Inn at General Lee's Headquarters.

Are there any soldiers buried under the rooms occupied in the clean, modern motels in Gettysburg? It is doubtful. Yet, unexplainable events have occurred and continue to occur in the places where modern tourists sleep so comfortably and seemingly safe. Two letters I received confirm what may be an example of attempts to communicate from the Other World.

In 2008, a man and his family had taken a Ghosts of Gettysburg Candlelight Walking Tour® that informs visitors of the paranormal happenings along Seminary Ridge. His son's camera yielded a number of "orbs" taken at the site. At the end of the tour, they merely had to walk across the street to their motel, the Quality Inn at General Lee's Headquarters on Buford Avenue. Once they arrived at their room, a friend who had been travelling with them jokingly said, "Knock on wood, no ghosts in here," and he knocked on the wall. Although it was after midnight, they immediately heard knocking on the wall, as if in response to their rapping. The writer was afraid he might have to apologize for awakening their neighbor in the motel, yet, after a minute or so, the rapping stopped.

The next morning he spoke about the rapping noises to the maid who was making up his room. She told him that the week before, the guests in the room next to his complained to the desk about knocking on the wall in the middle of the night and hearing men's voices in the room where the knocking had originated. The next morning, when they went to the motel office to complain, they were told that no one had occupied the room next to them the night before. The writer inspected the room, and discovered that there was not only no neighbor on the side from where the knocking came, but no room. The room they had occupied was the last one in the row of motel rooms.

Photo Courtesy of Darlene Perrone

Six months later a woman and her family were renting the General Lee Suite on the second floor of the historic Widow Thompson's House, used by Robert E. Lee for planning part of the battle as his headquarters. The first night in the suite the woman was awakened several times by a loud knock or bang on the wall next to her bed and the sound of the doorknob turning as if someone were entering. At first she thought it might have been someone from her family who were in other parts of the suite. But when she arose to see, she realized that all the rest of the people in the suite were sound asleep.

Later her five-year-old son woke her up to tell her that he was seeing a face on the wall at the foot of the bed. She looked and saw nothing, and chalked it up to the imagination of a child.

The next night she was awakened again by the loud knocks on the wall and the doorknob turning. She also heard another strange, out-of-place sound: a woman humming to herself. Determined to prove to the others that the sounds were real and that she was not imagining them, she bought a digital recorder and recorded the entire last night of their visit. Upon playback, the machine had recorded the usual night sounds—snoring, rolling over in bed—but also the sounds she had heard of knocking on the walls and the doorknob turning. Then, about an hour into the recording, she suddenly heard, very plainly, a loud human voice say "Hi!"

What came next on the recording defies reality…but not the historical record. It is well known that Lee had several meals at the Thompson House, and that, when he was not riding the battle lines he received officers either in his tents across the road or in the home of the Widow Thompson. Although Lee's official staff was minimal, there was protocol to be followed and visitors must be announced.

Shortly after the first recording of a human voice there came another, a different voice, much lower and more formal than the first. Amazingly, it says, "General Lee will be with you."

The question remains: was this the remnant voice of Walter Taylor, Charles Marshall, or another of Lee's aides, somehow captured by the quartz-infused granite fieldstone walls of the Thompson House and suddenly played back because of some as yet unknown circumstances?

The greater question remains: If voices can somehow be recorded by the materials of an historical site itself, then what are the exact scientific circumstances needed to cause them to "replay" at our beck and call?

Answer that and you will have solved one of the great mysteries of the universe.

GETTYSBURG'S SECRETS

The dead! Why can't the dead die!
—Eugene O'Neill, *The Haunted, Act III*

During the first three days of July 1863, there were well over 175,000 men scattered over an area approximately 7 miles long by 5 miles wide, from Oak Hill, north of the town of Gettysburg to Big Round Top, from Herr's Ridge to East Cavalry Battlefield. In fact, there were probably many more men in the general vicinity of the small town of Gettysburg than that. Along with the combat troops, there were numerous support troops—doctors and orderlies, muleskinners, wagon masters and rear-echelon troops—as well as thousands of "body servants"—usually African-Americans—accompanying individual soldiers from the north and the south.

Since the town of Gettysburg sits smack in the middle of that acreage, of course soldiers moved through the town and stopped within its limits. On June 26, 1863, Confederates under General Jubal Early marched through Gettysburg on their way eastward; on the evening of June 30, Union cavalry under General John Buford rode through the town serenaded by young Gettysburg maidens; the next morning, Union Army infantry tramped through Gettysburg, serenaded by enemy rifle and artillery fire to the west and north of town; a few hours later these same troops retreated rapidly through the same streets upon which they advanced, followed by Confederates firing at them from just a block away.

A few nasty rear-guard actions took place within the town limits, at Mr. Kuhn's brickyard in the northeast quadrant of town and near the intersection of Chambersburg Street and Washington Street. Artillery set up on some of the slight rises on Carlisle Street and fired at the advancing rebels coming from the north. Men were shot down in the very streets where tourists drive their cars or stroll the sidewalks. Soldiers peered out from behind the corners of the buildings where visitors' children now place their small hands.

A Confederate flag was planted in the center square—the "Diamond"—in town, and, farther south at the corner of Breckenridge Street and Baltimore Street, after they advanced that far, a "rubble barricade" was erected behind which the southerners took pot-shots at Yankees down Baltimore Street who dared to move into view. It may have been from behind this barricade that

Jennie Wade was accidentally shot by some Confederate perhaps checking the windage on his rifle around 8:00, Friday morning, July 3.

After the first day's fight, some 25 Confederate regiments ended up within the current borough limits. And, of course, hundreds (if not thousands) of wounded were carried or made their way to the many "field hospitals" installed in the large public buildings and many of the smaller private dwellings in town.

So it is no wonder that, when a tourist arrives in Gettysburg for the first time and, expecting to see an area enclosed in a cyclone fence, asks, "Where's the battlefield?" he is answered with the seemingly smart-aleck answer, "You're standing on it."

While the town may not contain the same amount of acreage as the government-owned National Park, add to it the acreage of Gettysburg College and the Lutheran Seminary (both "battlefields") and it comes close. As well, while the National Park contains numerous buildings that were there during the battle, the town retains some 200 of the original 400 structures that witnessed the battle, far more than what is contained in the Park boundaries.

So, if human emotional energy and early, sudden death are some of the criteria for a site to be haunted, the town of Gettysburg would certainly qualify as much as any part of the National Park.

It is no wonder then, that, over the years, I have received a number of letters from current and former residents of Gettysburg who have experienced unexplainable happenings in their tidy homes in Gettysburg.

In *Ghosts of Gettysburg VI*, I wrote of a woman who grew up in Gettysburg and told the story of how she and her grade school chums ended up in the cellar of an abandoned house on the north side of Gettysburg and discovered a "tunnel" which ran off in a southerly direction. A local Gettysburg policeman confirmed the rumors of an "underground Gettysburg" and reminded me of the tales of tunnels beneath the Catholic Church. While I believe the individuals to be credible, still, I myself have never seen or entered one of these subterranean warrens. But because of letters I have been sent, they must be more than mere rumors.

A number of Gettysburgians recall rumors of tunnels under the streets, some going back to Prohibition days, some even further. One businessman assumed that they might have been used to transport goods—legal or illegal—between buildings. It was easier to go from one underground storage area to another via a tunnel than to carry goods upstairs, through a shop, outside, through the other shop and back downstairs. It also kept busy-body neighbors from speculating on what was going on.

Tunnels on Virginia plantations are extremely common. The urban legend is that they were constructed in case of Indian attack: the family could escape to the nearby river and a waiting boat. More likely, since many of the plantation houses were built high above the river, the tunnels were used to transport goods from ships on the river to the cellars or cold storage "dependencies"—out-buildings—more easily than cutting an unsightly road from the river to the main house.

Several years ago I received a letter from a woman who lived in Gettysburg on the south side of the first block of Chambersburg Street from July 1960 until March 1961. Her apartment was on the second floor. From it she could see a tavern across the street. She recalled that during her stay she experienced cold spots in the apartment. She had also heard doors open and close when there was no one but her there. One time, when she was the only one living there, she opened her door to the hall and saw footprints where someone had walked on the rug outside her door. There had been none a few minutes before.

She must have been somewhat psychically sensitive. During the time she was living in Gettysburg, she claims she could hear screams emanating from the battlefield. (She would not have been the only one to hear battle-related noises where there should not be any. Others have heard cannons being fired and the "rattle" of musketry. Once, at the Triangular Field, I heard a drummer tap just one measure of a rhythm. Then there are the ancient rumors of farmer Forney's workers hearing orders shouted, bugles being blown, bullets thumping into flesh, and the screams of men in mortal terror. The place these things were heard: Iverson's Pits.)

Late one night she and her neighbor heard someone walk down the hall and descend the stairs that led to the basement. The neighbor's husband accompanied them as they followed the sound to the basement. They heard the steps lead to the back of the underground room. As they followed the sound they ended up in front of an old, small door. Although there was no sign of whomever it was that made the sounds of footsteps, they opened the door. It led to a small tunnel that ran directly under Chambersburg Street and came up on the tavern side of the street. They could distinctly hear the cars rumbling overhead, and were a bit confused. Although they apparently followed a person into the tunnel, cobwebs from low ceiling to floor and from side-to-side were still intact. Yet this is where they heard the person go.

An unexplainable fear suddenly struck all three and they hurried back. They were later told that the tunnel was used for the Underground Railroad. Gettysburg was indeed a stop on the Underground Railroad.

The Alexander Dobbin House, now one of Gettysburg's finer restaurants, has always been known as a "station" on the Underground Railroad. There is a small area near the reservation desk that visitors can peer into and see the cramped accommodations reserved for the escaping slaves. (It is interesting since the Reverend Dobbin was known to have owned slaves himself.)

Research on the topic of the Underground Railroad is especially difficult because of the clandestine nature of the endeavor. Written records were rarely kept and everything was in code: There were "conductors" and "station masters," "depots" and "stations" and "tracks," using railroad references for trusted helpers, safe stops along the route, and the route itself. "Stockholders" in the Underground Railroad were those individuals who gave money. Directions were given orally or memorized in song: The old slave song, "Follow the Drinkin' Gourd," was a reference to the Big Dipper in the sky which would point the night travelers always northward. Some historians think they may have discovered coded directions in quilts, made by Abolitionists right under the noses of slaveholders, and hung out on the clothesline to guide escaping slaves.

Slaves crossing the Mason-Dixon Line on the Baltimore Pike into Gettysburg were told to go to the first stream (Rock Creek), turn right and find the mill. The mill was McAllister's Mill, owned by some Gettysburg Abolitionists who would hide the runaways in the "cog-pit," under the mill, an unlikely place for "paterollers" (patrollers—slave catchers) to look.

The reason so few written records were kept is because the law of the land made criminals out of individuals with conscience. Several Fugitive Slave Laws had been passed over the years, but the Fugitive Slave Act of 1793 made assisting escapees a punishable crime. The act passed in 1850 toughened the law.

Some excellent research on this difficult topic was done by historian and teacher Craig Caba. He discovered a Pennsylvania College fraternity house, now gone, on East Middle Street, across from the old G.A.R. Hall, which apparently housed an abolitionist-oriented brotherhood. The "Beta Deltas" or "Black Ducks" would be awakened in the middle of the night by a knock on the door and a voice informing them that "Jim"—probably a code name for an escaped slave—was at the back door. They would house him there or move him to a cave-like geological formation on Culp's Hill, cryptically named "Number 33," to feed him and await further instructions. It would not surprise me if there was a tunnel under East Middle Street, especially since the G.A.R. building was once a church.

In Gettysburg, the question remains: If underground Gettysburg is laced with tunnels, what was their purpose and who built them?

And perhaps a better question is: What entities may still use those tunnels as entrances to our very domiciles, and what are *their* purposes?

INVESTIGATING THE UNKNOWN

Searchers after horror haunt strange, far places.

–H. P. Lovecraft

It's one thing, on a dark night, in a known haunted venue, to accidentally run into an entity from another world; it's yet another to seek them out, to purposefully enter their world with its bizarre rules, to taunt them, to antagonize them to come from whatever plane upon which they toil and rest and play, to show themselves, in whatever form they choose.

Most people visit Gettysburg during the summer. They fight the crowds to have meals, stand in lines to visit attractions, jostle for parking spaces on Little Round Top and other battlefield sites, and take ghost tours in droves.

Spring and fall are nice times to visit as many parents and alumni of Gettysburg College can attest. But weekends can still be a hassle, since all the events—Alumni Weekend, Parents Weekend, Homecoming, the famous Adams County Apple Harvest and Apple Blossom Festivals—are all held on weekends.

But during the "off-season" in Gettysburg, things are pretty slow. After Remembrance Day weekend, commemorating the anniversary of Lincoln's Gettysburg Address in mid-November, most of the attractions close or abbreviate their hours, and none of the seasonal programs is presented. Gettysburg becomes just another small, wintry town until the school groups on their obligatory class trips to Gettysburg, begin arriving again in the spring.

And while the tourists to Gettysburg are warmly ensconced in their homes and the people in the tourist industry are relaxing after attempting to satisfy every tourist's whim for eight or nine months, the ghosts are still active. They never get a vacation.

While winter may not be a good time to take a ghost walking tour it is a very good time to conduct paranormal investigations in and around Gettysburg. There are very few visitors to "contaminate" photos or electronic voice phenomena recordings. (Don't even bother to attempt to collect "EVP" on a night in July in Devil's Den—there's way too much noise from kids running around and their parents attempting to round them up. You won't be able to tell the EVP rebel yell from the shouts of the visitors.) But during the winter, much of the battlefield, as well as the town, are as deserted as a…well, ghost town.

One good thing about owning a haunted Civil War era building—the Ghosts of Gettysburg Tour Headquarters—is that I can "lock it down" for paranormal experiments any time I want. For example, I have often wondered what effect the human component has on gathering EVP. I've always thought that energy is needed in order for paranormal entities to manifest. That's why batteries in equipment often die during paranormal investigations; that, I believe, is why I am completely exhausted after just an hour-long EVP session. Although I have always insisted that I am not psychically sensitive, that apparently doesn't matter to entities when they need energy—they steal it from me.

Normally, in collecting EVP, I will ask a question while holding the recorder (set on "voice activation mode") in my hand, wait 30-40 seconds before I ask another question, then repeat the procedure. Although I have placed the recorder on a surface and still gotten EVP, I've always wondered, how much EVP could the recorder collect by itself? Will the entities have enough energy without a living being present to impress their personalities on the recorder? How much a factor is the haunted venue on the collection of EVP?

One cold winter night I placed the recorder in what I consider the most paranormally active room in the house, turned it on and walked out. The next morning I retrieved it. When I looked at the digital counter, I was astounded. With no one in the room, the recorder started at 3:55 A.M. and captured 44 minutes of EVP. As well, at least twice during the snowy night snowplows passed "The Ghost House," so you can hear "real" noise to compare it with the EVP. Raspy roars, clicks, whistles, whispers, "white noise," and murmuring, sounding very much like a serene gathering of souls in the background can be heard throughout the 44 minutes. So much for needing my energy for ghosts to impress themselves upon the digital recorder.

During another investigation at the ante-bellum Needwood Mansion near Rockville, Maryland, I was attempting to get EVP while another investigator videotaped me in near infra-red. My opinion of "orbs" is that 95% of them are dust, insects, or moisture too close to the lens and thus appearing as out-of-focus circles. As I held the recorder in my hand, the video showed "orbs" gathering to the recorder, coming out of the wall, out of a mirror, and out of thin air, apparently acting in an intelligent manner, approaching the recorder to impress their message. As I was playing the recording, the orbs began to gather again, as if they wanted to hear themselves. I have to conclude that, while many "orbs" are just naturally occurring contaminants, some display intelligence and must be something else.

Owning a haunted house also means that I am aware of virtually all the spots where equipment will give a false positive reading. For example, I can guarantee that someone with an EMF meter will find a ghost under the bed on the second floor—if the ceiling fan on the floor below is operating. A ghost can also be detected by an EMF meter in that room…when the refrigerator motor in the next room starts. Obviously, these are not ghosts being detected, but naturally occurring anomalies generated by the house itself.

And yet there are those times when the ghosts come and make their presence undeniably known.

One night during an investigation, I had led the group into the back room on the second floor, the room I used for the EVP experiment. One man was sitting in a chair behind me. He had been using the EMF meter with great success at the other sites we had investigated that day. I was attempting to gather EVP. The room was exceptionally quiet. Suddenly his EMF meter began to beep, registering a very high EMF presence. I turned to him, expecting him to have directed the probe toward a known "hot spot." I asked him, "Did you move the probe?" He had the device still on his lap and shook his head. The EMF meter continued to react to an unseen electromagnetic force that seemed to strengthen and weaken over the course of three or four minutes. He still hadn't moved the probe. Then, just as suddenly as it had begun, it stopped.

We all agreed that, since he wasn't moving the probe, the electromagnetic force was coming to him. And that just doesn't happen normally. It happens paranormally.

Periodically, someone will contact me, saying they've been having paranormal activity in their building. After initial contacts are made, we conduct a preliminary investigation. I interview the owner and percipients of the activity. My wife, Carol, and one of our trusted mediums will go around the building, picking up paranormal "hot spots." After they're finished, we all get together. More often than not, the owner is stunned by the information the medium has gathered, much of which backs up what the owner had just been telling me.

Often, this first pass through the haunted site will help the owner and family to understand that there is really nothing to fear from their ghosts. It also helps us to determine whether or not a property needs a full investigation. If it does, we pull together a team of photographers, videographers, a medium or two, and bring equipment such as EMF meters, quick-read thermometers and motion-sensitive, infra-red cameras to leave overnight. Hopefully, we'll gather more evidence to assure the homeowner and the family that their ghosts are benign. Sometimes our mediums will help the spirits "cross over," if that indeed is what they (the spirits) wish to do. If, on the rare occasion, there is a troublesome entity, we'll deal with it and give the owners hints on how to handle it should it return.

Our paranormal investigation team was recommended to a production company associated with the Travel Channel, and so, in 2008, the Ghosts of Gettysburg team was featured on the Travel Channel's *Mysterious Journeys* television series. The series featured several of the most mysterious places in the world. Of course, Gettysburg was featured for its ghosts. Our team investigated for the cameras six haunted sites in and around Gettysburg including the Cashtown Inn, the Gettysburg and Northern Railroad engine house, the Gettysburg Hotel, The Baladerry Inn, The Daniel Lady Farm and, of course, our own "Ghost House."[1]

Because of the notoriety the program brought, we decided to make use of our "down time" in the winter and offer Mysterious Journeys Weekends to the general public. The idea is that those interested in doing something a little beyond your regular ghost tour can spend a weekend in Gettysburg and do paranormal investigations of some of the sites they saw on television with the team they saw on TV. Fortunately, the historic (and haunted!) Cashtown Inn agreed to be a part of the weekends. The weekends never fail to provide some unexplainable happenings. They also give us an opportunity to investigate specific sites more than once to determine if paranormal activity—the ghosts—come and go and if they are more active at certain times than others.

They also provide some fine examples of paranormal investigations.

The weekend begins with a meet and greet at the Cashtown Inn on Friday afternoon. Usually, the Ghosts of Gettysburg Team consists of my wife Carol and me, Investigative Medium Laine Crosby, author and paranormal investigator Patty Wilson, and Scott Crownover, described on the Travel Channel as our "Tech Guru," although his expertise goes far beyond just the technical aspects of ghost hunting. Occasionally we're joined by other experts such as Rosemary Ellen Guiley, author of 34 books, including encyclopedias of various paranormal subjects and Ken Biddle, author of the book, *Dust or Orbs*.

We introduce the team, explain a few things about the weekend and some of the investigative techniques we'll be using, then sit down to an outstanding meal served by the Cashtown Inn. (If you've never eaten there, it has one of the finest restaurants in Pennsylvania—if not the entire East Coast.) After dinner, the owners, Jack and Maria Paladino, regale the investigators with ghost stories of the Cashtown Inn, which are numerous and chilling. Jack tells stories of when they first bought the place, of standing at the sink and being physically shoved out of the way by an unseen heavy hand; of a worker staying in the inn's upper rooms and hearing boot-steps outside in the hall, his locked door shake, then feeling the bed depress next to him; of inn guests hearing mysterious banging with no obvious source, going on in the halls.

Then we are allowed to investigate the cellar of the inn. (I say allowed because, with the exception of our Mysterious Journeys events, virtually no one is allowed into the cellar.) The lights go out, and our guests investigate the five rooms in the cellar beneath the Inn.

In the cellar I have captured a face peering into the window from the outside. The area where any living person could have been is inaccessible: it's under the porch and enclosed with latticework. But more impressive is the unfailing EVP that I consistently capture in that cellar.

Face in Basement Window

A quick history reveals the Cashtown Inn goes back to the late 18th Century. It has always served the public as a wayside tavern and carriage stop. During the second year of the Civil War, Confederate General J.E.B. Stuart rode by with his cavalrymen, raiding into Pennsylvania. A year later, the Inn became a focal point for the entire invading Confederate Army under General Robert E. Lee as they marched through Pennsylvania. General A. P. Hill had his headquarters there; Lee stopped and cut a map of the county from a door in Cashtown (probably the Inn's door since it was the most prominent building in Cashtown and we know Lee visited there). It was from Cashtown that Lee heard the sound of the guns at Gettysburg, seven miles to the east, and gave orders for his army to assemble at the small crossroads town whose name would be forever engraved in American History as the site of the saving of the Union and Lee's Waterloo.

One of the first casualties from the battle—a Confederate soldier who was "bushwacked" by some locals—was brought to the Inn and died. After the battle a large number of wounded were housed, and operated upon there, and the Confederate wagon train of wounded, which strung out for 17 miles, ponderously passed the Inn. Those who died in the vicinity were buried on the grounds. In the years since the battle, the Inn continued to serve the public. In the 1950s and 60s it was one of the more infamous biker bars in the area. (In fact, one of the patrons from that period still visits—long after his death!) In the 1980s it was turned into one of the finer Bed and Breakfasts in the area.

During one of our Mysterious Journeys Weekends, I collected an EVP recording in the cellar of a southern soldier answering the question as to what state he hailed from: "Miss-i-ssi-ppi" in four distinct syllables. Participants have gotten chills, weird, unexplainable photos, and "feelings" that they need to leave the cellar immediately. I, myself, have been touched on the shoulder blade—three times—in that cellar when no one—no one living, that is—was anywhere near me. After our cellar investigation, Scott Crownover analyzes the EVP obtained and explains the techniques he uses in his analysis. Everyone retires to their rooms to begin their own investigation of the Inn.

One night Scott and I placed a Bushnell, infrared "gamecam" in the bar of the Cashtown Inn. We knew that Jack locks the bar every night after he closes so it would be secured until morning. The nice thing about the gamecam is that you don't have to stay up all night to capture any activity. As well, everything is time-stamped. The next morning when we examined the camera, at 35 minutes after midnight, there's a bright, human-shaped figure moving past the "trip zone." It's a great picture of Jack as he is finishing locking the bar. Then, at 44 minutes after midnight, there is another figure that trips the camera. No one was in the locked bar when the photo was taken. There is no explanation—no "normal" explanation—as to what the image is.

Jack Locking the Bar   *Unknown Entity*

During one preliminary investigation, Scott, Patty, Carol, a film crew and I went into the first room on the right at the top of the stairs. We no sooner entered the room than all the women announced that they smelled strong cigarette smoke. Odd, since the Cashtown Inn is completely smoke-free. Odder still because the men in the room smelled nothing. The three women were amazed because they smelled it so strongly. Patty began to piece together, from what she was receiving, a strong male personality nicknamed "Sarge." He had been a veteran of two wars, Korea and Vietnam; he had been a regular at the Cashtown Inn when it was a biker bar; he rode a motorcycle. Patty asked what kind of motorcycle he rode, then commented that she thought he was a Native American. I asked why she thought that and she answered that he had said "Indian." I told her that in the 1950s and 60s, before the Harley Davidson revolution, the most popular American bike was named "Indian." It seemed that the entity was a bit of a prankster with a sense of humor. He refused to give us his name. He said he wanted a young, pretty girl to talk to, so the next day we brought our 28 year-old daughter to the Inn. He was apparently pleased, because it was then we found out his name was "John."

On Saturday of Mysterious Journeys Weekends we have breakfast at the Cashtown Inn and have our guests summarize what happened during their previous night. We've been told stories ranging from lights flashing outside the Inn to strange, unexplainable noises with no apparent source. Jack sits in and tries to explain what the events might have been. More often than not, he is at a loss. During a recent Mysterious Journeys Weekend guests from several rooms in the old section of the Inn heard what they described as banging—like rifle-butts being slammed on the floor in unison as if during a drill—below their rooms. One of them counted over thirty bangs. An investigation provided no explanation. The next night, the same sound was heard in both sections of the Inn. Over forty slamming sounds were heard throughout the building by several of the participants. No source was ever discovered.

Lunch is on their own and our attendees discover some of the wonderful places to eat in Gettysburg. Afterward we meet back at the Inn and head out to our first investigation site, the Gettysburg and Northern Railroad Engine House, which sits on a part of Gettysburg's first day's battlefield not owned by the National Park Service. The engine house is another site exclusive to our investigation team. Two hour investigations there have yielded numerous EVPs including communication from "Em" who was originally very loud, so loud as to make the EVP unintelligible. Finally, I asked "Em" if she could talk a little more quietly. Upon playback, in front of a number of skeptical railroad executives, a female voice whispered, "I'll be quiet." On later investigations, a road safety barrel was forcibly kicked by an unseen foot from a tire upon which it was resting and footsteps on an engine were heard by everyone in the group. The sounds of someone invisible walking lasted for eight minutes. I asked the manager if that engine might be cooling off and contraction of the metal the cause for the noises. He replied that the engine had been parked there for a month and was drained of all liquids.[2]

Next we caravan to the Daniel Lady Farm, also normally off limits to other paranormal investigators. This historic farm was the encampment site for Johnson's Confederate Division and where General Robert E. Lee visited. After their evening assault on July 2, the wounded of Johnson's Division came streaming back and the barn and house were used as bloody field hospitals, witnessing hundreds of amputations, deaths and burials. Investigations of the barn, surrounding fields and house have supplied many EVPs and more than a few strange photos.[3] Behind the barn during a night investigation, my sleeve was forceably pulled. I turned to confront the perpetrator and found no one behind me. In the house, the operating room's energy seems to come and go, occasionally being so strong as to force more sensitive—and even some not so sensitive—in the group to leave the area.

The final investigation is of the Ghosts of Gettysburg Candlelight Walking Tours® Headquarters, a structure that dates back to 1834. There are several "resident" ghosts, including the feisty Mrs. Kitzmiller, who owned the house longer than anyone right after the battle, several soldiers from Georgia who may have been wounded and brought to the house, and "Hank," a Louisiana soldier who goes on duty after the lights are turned off. At least two children's spirits remain in the house. In a recent experiment, they moved pendulums on a rack while setting off an EMF meter (all recorded on video, of course). Members of our group have been pushed by invisible children, the bathroom door handle has been jiggled by tiny, unseen hands, and three distinct footsteps were heard by myself and group members coming down the wooden steps...and everyone in the group was already downstairs! Mrs. Kitzmiller, a proper Victorian lady, tells our mediums she's upset that Carol doesn't put out cookies and tea for our guests, not realizing that in modern times, without a food license, that might be illegal. After Carol put out some tiny wafer cookies as a gesture, I asked Mrs. Kitzmiller, how she liked the cookies. The EVP was adamant: "I hate them," a disembodied voice said.

Sunday morning is spent summing up everyone's experiences over breakfast. It seems that even diehard skeptics in the group must admit that there is something going on. As one skeptical gentleman put it: "I don't believe in ghosts...but they scared the hell out of me!"

ENDNOTES

What's Left of Camp Letterman

1 Except for Gregory Coco. As a park ranger he often gave a living history demonstration as a surgeon and his descriptions were some of the most graphic one could imagine. I suppose his philosophy was much like mine: how will we ever stop warfare if we don't understand how horrible it is.

2 Gregory Coco's book, *A Strange and Blighted Land*, is one of the best sources for information on the wounded and their care after the battle. But, once again, figures vary widely as far as numbers of men treated and released, the number of tents, the exact location of the graveyard, and so forth.

3 Dr. Janusz Slawinski, in "The Journal of Near Death Studies" concluded that the dying human body releases about 1,000 times the normal 12 watts of electricity it constantly produces. He named this 12,000 watts of bioelectricity released at death a "light shout." Found in Melvin Morse, M.D. *Transformed by the Light*, Ballantine Books, 1992.

All the King's Horses

1 Some sources report that, on the morning of July 1, 1863, at Gettysburg, the advancing Confederates stopped and formed "hollow squares," the standard defense against attacking cavalry. This leads us to believe that Buford had ordered at least one mounted attack as a feint or a delaying tactic, then rescinded the order. In fact, in a paper on the first day at Gettysburg by Major E. P. Halstead (reprinted in *The Gettysburg Papers*, by Ken Bandy and Florence Freeland, Vol. I, p. 156), he states that Buford, after fighting all morning and retreating to west of the Evergreen Cemetery, "moved his command out in plain view of the enemy and formed for a charge; the enemy, seeing the movement, formed squares in echelon." The feint helped the First Corps to escape, but the controversy whether the Confederates formed squares continued until 1885.

2 See my book *Saber and Scapegoat: J. E. B. Stuart and the Gettysburg Controversy* for an account of the cavalry during the Gettysburg Campaign and the fight at East Cavalry Field.

3 James Donovan, *A Terrible Glory: Custer and the Little Bighorn, The Last Great Battle of the American West*, pp. 46-47.

How to Un-Haunt a House

1 A more complete discussion of the case, including expert commentary, is found in *The Encyclopedia of Ghosts and Spirits* Second Edition, by Rosemary Ellen Guiley, pp. 82-83.

2 His spirit went on to cause severe poltergeist activity in the house, including kitchen appliances moving, dishes being thrown about, and loud blasts of sound coming from the room where he had been trapped. See *Ghosts of Gettysburg III*, "The Premature Burial," pp.11-14, for the entire story of the house cleansing.

3 All of these stories in detail are documented in the *Ghosts of Gettysburg* book series of 6 volumes.

4 See *Ghosts of Gettysburg IV*, "Sleepers, Awake!"

Dark Night of the Soul

1 Cathi Schue, former president of the GBPA collected much of the history of the Daniel Lady Farm and has worked tirelessly for over a decade raising funds, researching, scraping, painting, pointing and literally hauling trash from the site. The Lady Farm would certainly not be the jewel it is today without her efforts.

2 The Gettysburg Battlefield Preservation Association is a non-profit, membership and donation driven organization with no paid staff, thereby allowing all donated funds and membership dues to go directly to preservation. Information on memberships and tax-deductible donations can be obtained by inquiry to the GBPA, Box 4087, Gettysburg, PA 17325.

The Bridge of Sighs

1 For another ghost story concerning Sachs Bridge, see *Ghosts of Gettysburg IV*, pp. 56-62, "The Bridge to Nowhere."

2 Another investigator, also astounded at her refusal, asked her later what had happened. Karyol said she felt as if she were standing in a vortex and felt light-headed. She said she felt she didn't have the energy at that point "to deal with the energy there." The investigator remembered Karyol saying that it took more of her energy to deal with evil than it did to deal with good. Perhaps that was why she felt compelled to leave the bridge at that moment.

3 I am skeptical of all amateur "ghost investigators." Rick Fisher and others have set up strict protocols when it comes to investigations that accomplish much to eliminate "false" readings and photographs. They include removing camera straps so they won't show up as "ghosts," not smoking while taking pictures, not taking photos in the rain or snow, placing motion detectors on

a solid object and not holding them in your moving hand, and other common sense, but often overlooked methods. Historical research is a large part of an investigation. Uninitiated people will go to a site without having done research, smoke, take pictures in foul weather, and are excited (and misled) when they see "orbs," in their photos. Therefore, any investigators I mention in my books are well aware of the protocols and act accordingly on their investigations.

Tales from the Guides
[1] Not her real name.
[2] Not her real name.
[3] Not his real name.
[4] For most of the stories see, *Ghosts of Gettysburg VI*, by Mark Nesbitt
[5] Not her real name.

The Ghost Train
[1] In September 2010, I too was a victim of the mysterious "boom" that rocked the car and shook the earth below it. Again, inspection of the outside of the car revealed nothing that could have caused the loud noise.

More Mysteries on Oak Ridge
[1] See Mark Nesbitt, "The Mysteries of Oak Ridge" in *Ghosts of Gettysburg V.*
[2] "The First Army Corps on the First Day at Gettysburg," Address by George W. Grant, First Lieutenant, Eighty-Eighth Pennsylvania Infantry, *The Gettysburg Papers* Vol. I., p. 261.
[3] Gregory Coco, *A Strange and Blighted Land*, p. 71.
[4] Grant, p. 263.
[5] www.gdg.org/research/OOB/Union/July 1-3/gpaul.html. Also www.ancestry.com.
[6] Peripheral vision of the human eye apparently is more sensitive to the frequencies of the paranormal than straight-on vision. Many people have reported seeing ghosts out of the corner of their eye, then when they try to focus, the vision vanishes.
[7] Phone interview with Christine Thomas, 2/15/2008.

General Lee's Headquarters
[1] Timothy Smith's small book on Lee's Headquarters, is typical of all his historical work: extremely well researched and fascinating in its detail. It is highly recommended to anyone interested in the complete history of the site.

Investigating the Unknown

1 The series is broadcast periodically or available on YouTube for anyone interested in its content.

2 For a fuller description of strange paranormal events that have been documented at the engine house, see the chapter entitled "The Ghost Train" in this volume.

3 For a more detailed version of happenings at the Daniel Lady Farm, see the chapter entitled "Dark Night of the Soul" in this volume.

Mark Nesbitt was born in Lorain, Ohio, and graduated from Baldwin-Wallace College with a BA in English Literature. He worked for the National Park Service as a Ranger/Historian for five years and then became a Licensed Battlefield Guide. During his tenure with the National Park Service, he had the opportunity to spent time in nearly every historic house on the Park and actually lived in four of the historic homes. Living in Gettysburg since 1971 has given him a unique "insider" perspective from which to write this book.

Mr. Nesbitt published the first book in the popular *Ghosts of Gettysburg* series in 1991. The *Ghosts of Gettysburg* stories have been seen, and/or heard, on The History Channel, A&E, The Discovery Channel, The Travel Channel, Unsolved Mysteries, and Coast to Coast AM.

Other books in print and ebooks by Mark Nesbitt:
Ghosts of Gettysburg
More Ghosts of Gettysburg
Ghosts of Gettysburg III
Ghosts of Gettysburg IV
Ghosts of Gettysburg V
Ghosts of Gettysburg VI

Haunted Pennsylvania
The Big Book of Pennsylvania Ghost Stories

If the South Won Gettysburg
35 Days to Gettysburg: The Campaign Diaries of Two American Enemies(Reprinted as The Gettysburg Diaries: War Journals of Two American Adversaries)
Rebel Rivers: A Guide to Civil War Sites on the Potomac, Rappahannock, York, and James
Saber and Scapegoat: J.E.B. Stuart and the Gettysburg Controversy
Through Blood and Fire: The Selected Civil War Papers of Major General Joshua Chamberlain